S.R. Bissette's Blur
(Complete Edition)
Volume 3: Video Views
(2000-2001)

Also by Stephen R. Bissette

Aliens: Tribes
We Are Going to Eat You! The Third World Cannibal Movies
Comic Book Rebels (with Stanley Wiater)
The Monster Book: Buffy the Vampire Slayer
(with Christopher Golden, Thomas E. Sniegoski)
Prince of Stories: The Many Worlds of Neil Gaiman
(with Hank Wagner, Christopher Golden)

edited by Stephen R. Bissette
Taboo 1-9, Taboo Especial

Also from Black Coat Press:

S.R.Bissette's Blur Vol. 1
S.R. Bissette's Blur Vol. 2
Teen Angels: Rick Veitch's Brat Pack and the Art, Karma and Commerce of Killing Sidekicks

edited by Stephen R. Bissette

Green Mountain Cinema I:
Green Mountain Boys

S. R. Bissette's Blur
Volume 3: Video Views
(2000-2001)

by

Stephen R. Bissette

A Black Coat Press Book

S.R. Bissette's Blur (Complete Edition) Volume 2 and all its contents Copyright © 2000, 2001, 2008 Stephen R. Bissette. Cover illustration Copyright © 2008 by Stephen R. Bissette.

Cover design: Jon-Mikel Gates
Packaged by SpiderBaby Grafix & Publications.

To contact the author, please write to:
Stephen R. Bissette, PO Box 157, Windsor, VT 05089,
or visit:
www.srbissette.com

A complete set of the original *Brattleboro Reformer Arts & Entertainment* sections, featuring *Video Views* and my miscellaneous articles, and an almost-complete set of *VMag* are preserved in the Stephen R. Bissette Collection in the HUIE Library at Henderson State University in Arkadelphia, Arkansas. *The Reformer* is also accessible via microfiche at the Brooks Memorial Library in Brattleboro, VT.

Visit our website at www.blackcoatpress.com

ISBN 978-1-934543-57-3. First Printing November 2008. Published by Black Coat Press, an imprint of Hollywood Comics.com, LLC, P.O. Box 17270, Encino, CA 91416. All rights reserved. Except for review purposes, no part of this book may be reproduced or transmitted in any form or by any means, electronic or mechanical, including photocopying, recording or by any information storage and retrieval system, without permission in writing from the publisher. Printed in the United States of America.

For Mike:
Been Here,
Done That,
Still Doing This
Every Week

Acknowledgements:

These reviews and essays were originally published in *The Brattleboro Reformer*, *VMag*, *The Chicopee Herald* and *The Reminder*. Some were also presented, in revised and expanded form, in *The Video Watchdog*.

My thanks to my respective editors and publishers, particularly Chris Nixon (my first *Brattleboro Reformer Arts & Entertainment* editor), Willow Dannible (my second), and Jon Potter (the current *Reformer A&E* editor); Steve Murphy (*VMag* and a comrade-in-arms from my comics days/daze); G. Michael Dobbs (*The Chicopee Herald*, *The Reminder*, and the dearest and closest friend of 'em all); and to Tim and Donna Lucas, who accepted expanded versions of some of these reviews for inclusion in the pages of *The Video Watchdog*, all of which are properly cited herein. Whenever possible, I have included those revised versions, as they were always superior to the *Video Views* versions, if only for the gift of a bit more time for one more polish along with Tim's invaluable editorial insights and guidance.

Thanks to Alan Goldstein for asking me to tackle the column back in '99. Thanks to everyone at First Run Video, including our customers. Thanks, too, to the many fellow independent video store owners, members of the New England Buying Group, and the various studio reps who provided insights, opinions, and screeners whenever necessary, and often when they weren't necessary.

Special thanks to Jon-Mikel Gates for his considerable assistance with computer and information retrieval/rescue aid provided, and for his excellent cover design work.

Thanks to then-Marjory Bleier — now Marjory Bissette — who put up with me throughout this manic two year-plus saga and opened my eyes to the pleasures of films (and life) I might otherwise have skirted. Thanks to my then-teenage offspring Maia Rose and Daniel, for the same and so much more. Thanks also to Jen Vaughn and Joshua Rosen for their patient proofreading of the *Blur* volumes 3-5 manuscripts.

Finally, thanks to Jean-Marc and Randy Lofficier, who made these collections possible.

SRB

Introduction

FOCUS

Having gone on, in some length, in the introductions to *Blur Volume 1* and 2 about the whys, wherefores and particulars of this book series, I'll not belabor the point.

This book series, to the best of my abilities, archives every *Video Views* column I wrote between 1999 and 2001. Subsequent volumes (already in the works) will similarly archive my essays and film reviews for other venues.

As for the material archived in *Blur* volumes 1-4, a few of what follows were originally published as articles, but most were the regular weekly column.

Supplementing my digital files may, upon occasion, mean including work in later volumes that belonged, chronologically, in earlier volumes; in the end, in any case, *Blur* will indeed encompass my entire body of video review work, with the exception of pieces I choose to reserve for inclusion in the upcoming *Gooseflesh* volumes.

The Brattleboro Reformer was my regular weekly publisher. The *Video Views* columns began in the *Reformer*'s *Arts & Entertainment* (hereafter *A&E*) on September 9, 1999, and continued weekly thereafter through October of 2001. *Blur, Volume 1* collected every *Reformer Video View* column from that first entry to March

30, 2000; *Volume 2* collected the *Video View* columns from April to the end of October, 2000.

This collection continues that chronology, beginning in November 2000 and concluding with my initial May, 2001 two-part column on Dogme 95.

Blur, Volume 1 also included capsule reviews for *VMag* (which debuted in November 1997), edited and published by my friend Stephen Murphy.[1] leading into my first *Brattleboro Reformer* columns. My editor at the *Reformer A&E* section at that time was Chris Nixon; by the time of the reviews showcased in this third volume, Willow Dannible was my editor (by the period of time represented in this volume, former *A&E* editor Chris Nixon had moved on to greener pastures). I thank her again for the ongoing good relations and indulging my occasionally page-stretching extravaganzas. My good friend G. Michael Dobbs also occasionally published my column in his Massachusetts weeklies, *The Chicopee Herald* and *The Reminder*.[2]

The body of work showcased in this volume has one more source that must be gratefully acknowledged. By the winter of 2000-2001, more and more of my col-

---

[1] Despite my best efforts, the lack of original digital files and/or a complete set of *VMag* (neither I nor Steve Murphy have yet found a copy of the November 2000 issue) mean a definitive inventory of my *VMag* work was inconclusive at this writing. All references in this volume, however, are complete. If further material surfaces, I will incorporate it into future volumes of *Blur* for the sake of completion.

[2] Again, records about what was published when and where in Mike's newspapers is sketchy; despite Mike's best efforts, not every published piece was archived in my own files, and neither of us kept proper records. I've footnoted every publication in Mike's weeklies that I know of herein.

umns were being revised and expanded for publication in *The Video Watchdog*, edited and published by my good friends Tim and Donna Lucas. Whenever possible, I have included those revised versions herein, as they were always superior to the *Video Views* versions, if only for the gift of a bit more time for one more polish, and Tim's invaluable editorial insights and guidance. Thank you, Tim, and long may the *Watchdog* bark into the night.

The dates given before each column cite the original date of publication; on those occasions when unforeseen editorial decisions resulted in a column being 'bumped' to the following week or otherwise revised, I have preserved the chronology in which the columns were written (corresponding, by and large, with the respective video release dates), incorporating editorial alterations only when they improved or significantly altered the context of the published review. Longer columns were sometimes run as two-part pieces; those columns are specified as such with their respective publication dates, and annotated as necessary. As *Video Views* grew and reader response proved favorable, my editors seemed happy to indulge even my wildest schemes.

Unlike my ongoing writing for the horror film fan magazines (which will be collected in the book series *Gooseflesh*, also from Black Coat Press), I could not presume my readers knew anything about films or filmmakers. There was no communal shorthand I could rely upon. I was writing for an audience that *might* know who Alfred Hitchcock, Steven Spielberg, and George Lucas were, but maybe not. For most *Reformer* readers, only the big movie stars had any name value or instantly-identifiable celebrity. So I took it upon myself to remind readers in almost every column that individuals, artists, indeed made these movies, these videos, that filled the new release wall at First Run Video. I hoped to elevate the interest level in the medium by doing much more than write capsule reviews, but in doing so always had to be sure I provided constant reference points. Thus, I would cite other works by the same filmmakers, other films performers had appeared in, specify cinematic precursors and sources.

In the disposable forum of a weekly newspaper column, this wasn't intrusive, but once those columns are collected, the repetition of certain filmographies or references can seem rather dreary. Still, I have decided to run the columns as they originally were published. This may make these collections more useful for younger readers and neophyte film buffs, but I hope this aspect of the columns collected in this series won't prove too exasperating to the knowledgeable film aficionados who deign to dig into these writings.

I have also cross-referenced reviews published in *Blur, Volume 1* and *2*, and footnoted updates on the filmmakers interviewed for the *Video Views* columns that appear in this volume.

Another element of my life in the video industry, and specifically my work with First Run Video and the New England Buying Group during this period, manifests in these columns. What had begun with a couple of 1999-2000 guest appearances of filmmakers at our Brattleboro, Vermont video superstore (directors Jay Craven, Nora Jacobson, Stefan Avalos, and Lance Weiler; see *Blur, Volume 1* and *Green Mountain Cinema I*) grew into increasing contact with active, independent filmmakers seeking bridges to active, independent retailers. I was more than happy to lend a hand, building upon my personal experiences as a publisher and self-publisher who worked hard during my years in comics to construct similar ties with independent comics retailers. The issues were surprisingly similar, as were the industry dynamics, though they played out on a far vaster scale in the video industry.

My involvement with the Video Software Dealers Association (VSDA) and their initial *"Filmmakers of Tomorrow"* program (initiated in part by *The Last Broadcast* co-director Lance Weiler) led to more aggressive interaction with filmmakers whose work I gravitated to, and which we chose to carry in First Run Video. Hence, the reviews collected in this volume of films like *Delinquent, Waiting*, and *Nice Guys Sleep Alone*, and interview/articles with their respective creators — Peter Christian Hall, Stu Pollard, Patrick Hasson, John Stefanic, Will Keenan — are a key part of this volume. Thanks to these exchanges, I also met many other filmmakers, including Mark Tapio Kines, Rich Mauro, and Vince Mola, and made lasting friendships with a few, such as Lance Weiler and Stefan Avalos (more coverage of some of these filmmakers will appear in the *Gooseflesh* books). I only wish I could have done more bridge-building. For a time, this proved productive for everyone involved, and it's a pleasure to at last archive those efforts herein.

Looking back, through the process of compiling and polishing this series of books, I have to say I found many pleasant surprises. I had forgotten I'd seen, much less written about, many of these movies — hence the title of this book and book series.

Thankfully, it is no longer just a blur, consigned to yellowing newspapers and scattered magazines in my collection.

Enjoy.

2000

November 2:

FREQUENCY (2000): Many of Rod Serling's most compelling *Twilight Zone* episodes were grounded in a particularly contemporary American melancholy in which broken men found themselves inexplicably confronted with the fulfillment of their deepest wish to go back and change their lives... but of course, one must be careful what one wishes for.

Serling's moving *Twilight Zone* episode *"Walking Distance"* (the fourth in the series, originally broadcast on Oct. 30th, 1959), remains the best of these: an ad executive (Gig Young) out for a Sunday drive finds his home town exactly as it was when he was a child. Tragedy ensues when he confronts himself as a boy; wishing only to tell himself to savor his youth, the man causes an accident which almost cripples the lad, leaving the man with a limp he did not have before.

Serling excelled at crafting such elegant, eloquent parables in a mere half-hour. In this grand tradition (but clocking in at over two hours), *Frequency* builds its story on a similar wish-fulfillment fantasy, likewise grounded in nostalgia, regret, and a big *"what if."* What if a lonely, embittered man could reach back into the past and save his father's life, and thus save himself?

Police officer John Sullivan (Jim Caviezel of *The Thin Red Line*, 1998) is haunted by the childhood loss of his fireman father Frank (Dennis Quaid), who gave his life in a daring fire rescue attempt. While experimenting with his father's old short-wave radio, an unusually intense display of the Aurora Borealis causes the short-wave signal to span the thirty years that separate father and son, allowing John to speak to Frank on the eve of his death. The impossible wish is fulfilled — but by altering their shared past, John and Frank also change their future, sending unexpected shock waves through time.

Unlike Serling's prime *Twilight Zone* episodes, *Frequency* is not a parable; it is a thriller, first and foremost. It flirts with the resonance Serling habitually brought to such material, but the high-octane intensity 1990s Hollywood insists upon asserts itself and doesn't let up.

There have been a number of engaging films of late that entertained similar "what if" scenarios for women. *Sliding Doors* (1997), *Me, Myself, I* (1999), and *Passion of Mind* (2000) come immediately to mind, each exploring their respective parallel lives and possible futures with varying degrees of imagination and emotional substance; Christian Bale entertained similar *"what if"* notions in the modest British romance *Metroland* (1997). Of course, their American male counterparts in *Frequency* can't navigate such terrain without detouring into life-and-death mayhem, pitting brain and brawn against raging infernos and a canny serial killer. *Frequency* gets nervous whenever it approaches any real emotional candor: father and son bonding over baseball, bicycle riding, and a little heart-to-heart talk via the shortwave is safe turf, but the deeper implications are swept aside in the sometimes inventive action and suspense setpieces. These elements elbow their way into center stage as the film gains momentum. While this will satisfy many viewers, others will find it all a distraction from the core drama.

Toby Emmerich's script is constructed as a two-act suspenser, in which John first struggles to save his father's life; once they've accepted their unique situation, father and son must join forces across the span of three decades to solve a mystery and bring a killer to justice before they forfeit their lives. Thankfully, Jim Caviezel and Dennis Quaid sustain a believable father-and-son chemistry that lends heart to plot mechanics concerned only with keeping pulses racing. Caviezel and Quaid carry the day, and director Gregory Hoblit (*Primal Fear*, 1996, *Fallen*, 1998) keeps the pacing brisk enough to suspend audience disbelief through the increasingly tangled web of possible-future tangents.

Frequency occasionally creaks, strains, and falters, but it provides a lively evening's entertainment. En route, it plucks deeper chords which sets the film above most of its thriller contemporaries. Count your blessings and go for the ride. *(Rated "PG-13" for strong language, casual alcohol abuse, the forensic details of the murders, gunplay, and some violence.)*

The bonds between father, sons, and family during times of strife is also central to Mel Gibson's latest effort **THE PATRIOT** (2000). Gibson stars as Benjamin Martin, a former guerrilla fighter from the Colonial era's French/Indian wars who has retired his bloody ways to marry and raise a family. When British rule tightens inexorably as the Colonies assert their demand for freedom, widower Martin checks his instincts and remains neutral in hope of keeping his family out of the conflict until an overzealous British officer, Colonel Tavington (Jason Issacs), makes an example of Gibson's sons, slaying one and taking the eldest Gabriel (Heath Ledger of *10 Things I Hate About You*, 1999) prisoner. Quicker than you can spit, Gibson arms himself with his ol' tomahawk and sets off through the forest in pursuit, dispatching the unsuspecting Brits to free his elder son.

This opening sequence is irresistible, sparking an ancestral patriotic fervor, paternal devotion, and an almost primal sense of outrage and craving for retribution. Director Roland Emmerich (*Universal Soldier*, 1992, *Independence Day*, 1996, *Godzilla*, 1998, etc.) stages Martin's transformation from reluctant citizen and stern father to feral killer with intoxicating vigor. The urgency and danger are palpable, the father's need to rescue and retaliate sends our own blood racing. As Martin speeds through the woods like a predator, his younger sons bringing up the rear, the film rekindles the power of similar sequences in Michael Mann's marvelous *The Last of the Mohicans* (1992); when Martin tears into the last of the British infantry like a lycanthrope, flashing his blade and bathing in their blood, the film bares the nerve Clint Eastwood's magnificent *Unforgiven* (1992) exposed with the terrifying spectacle of a man shedding any semblance of civilized behavior, matching violence with unspeakable violence. With its electric immediacy and rugged sense of time and place, it is the drama, not the gore, that galvanizes us; this is potent stuff, and *The Patriot* is off and running.

Alas, the film fails to ever again approach such intensity. Gibson orchestrated similar historical raw materials into his rousing producer/director/star coup *Braveheart* (1995), and *The Patriot* shivers in the shadow of that true epic. Gibson and Ledger are charismatic players here, mustering engaging screen chemistry as father and son, and Issacs revels in the most cold-blooded screen villainy of the year, but Robert (*Saving Private Ryan*, 1998) Rodat's screenplay and Emmerich's direction fritter away their performances and the fiery rage of the opening act with flagging energy and invention. Martin's ragtag militia army outwits Tavington at every turn, but eventually succumb to their increasing isolation, dwindling supplies, and the extremities of Tavington's cruel butchery against their loved ones. By the final act, the militia falls into step with the very classical warfare traditions their guerrilla tactics so successfully ruptured in the first half of the film. Why? One grows increasingly weary of the sprawling battle scenes: why are the militia fighting on the *enemy's* terms? Though cannon balls decapitate soldiers and shear men in half, they do so each time to diminishing dramatic effect. We ache for the final confrontation between Martin and Tavington, but when it comes, we feel robbed. Martin has been provoked beyond all reason, been shorn of kith and kin, home and hearth, but we never again glimpse the monster of the first act we both dread and anticipate — and the climax, when it comes, rings hollow, lost amid the clamor of a poorly-executed battle.

As the Academy Award-winning director and star of *Braveheart*, Gibson proved he knows how to manage such a war with fearless clarity and vision; Emmerich fudges his American Revolutionary War to the point where we cease to care. Rodat and Emmerich shortchange their delicate effects, too: they establish the importance of the mother's star necklace as an icon, and effectively punctuate key narrative moments (such as Ledger's wedding) with the jewelry, but abandon the prop altogether when its cumulative power would be the greatest. Given the failed spectacle of the climax, such modest grace notes are sorely needed — but absent.

All in all, *The Patriot* recalls Andrew V. McLaglen's venerable War-Between-the-States saga *Shenandoah* (1965), which starred James Stewart as a family patriarch who also tries to remain neutral during a war that ravages his family as his sons join the fray and his daughter marries a confederate soldier. Stewart was great; the film wasn't (though I still have a soft spot in my skull for it). Like *Shenandoah*, *The Patriot* wants to be a full-blown epic, but it falls short. One cannot help but initially be swept up in the melodrama... and disappointed by its failure to deliver on its promise. Gibson gives *The Patriot* his best shot, matched by the villainy of Issacs and Tom Wilkinson (as Tavington's commanding officer General Cornwallis), but they are undermined by a script and direction that sags when it should soar. *(Rated "R" for war violence, gore, adult and sexual situations.)*

November 9:

Cards on the table: Though I am a great fan of director Brian De Palma's work, I hated DePalma's *Mission: Impossible* (1996), which eschewed the premise of the celebrated Bruce Geller TV series (seven seasons, 1966-73) from which the film lifted its title, catchy Lalo Schifrin title tune, and little else. Packaged as a star vehicle for co-producer Tom Cruise, the film's first act dispensed of the taut team performance that made the TV series so compelling, lurching from setpiece to backstabbing setpiece. In its *"who can you trust?"* paranoia, the most corruptive element was my utter distrust of the filmmakers. When you can trust neither the teller nor the tale, part of me checks out.

The film embodied all that's wrong with contemporary big-budget thrillers: in the era of CGI "action," the laws of physics exist only as a mere inconvenience. If anything is possible and the most rudimentary rules cease to apply, every action does not have its own equal and opposite reaction, fundamental logic is tossed out the window, and action ceases to have any meaningful consequences. Sans consequences, action ceases to matter. The *only* sequence that worked for me in the first *Mission Impossible* was the central caper, in which Cruise hung suspended over a high-security computer complex. For a moment, a drop of sweat threatened to give him away — and for a moment, just a moment, the rules of the physical world we ignore at our own peril meant something. As long as it served the filmmakers' need to manipulate us, gravity existed: if that drop of sweat dropped (and it would thankfully fall down, not up), Cruise's goose was cooked.

MISSION IMPOSSIBLE 2 (2000) — or, as its marketeers would have us call it, *MI2* — similarly suspends reality at whim, but for a time the shift in gears from the original film's betrayal-upon-betrayal narrative illogic is engaging. *MI2* isn't the shapeless beast the first film was. Screenplay writer Robert Towne (a long way from his superbly-crafted *Chinatown*, 1974) cobbles together a fresh persona for Ethan Hunt (Cruise) from a patchwork of elements lifted from Alfred Hitchcock's work and Ian Fleming's James Bond series. Savvy co-producer Cruise also corralled Hong Kong director John Woo (*The Killer*, 1989, *Hard-Boiled*, 1992, *Broken Arrow*, 1996, *Face/Off*, 1997) to helm this sequel, giving Woo free reign to (as *This is Spinal Tap* so eloquently put it) turn up the amplifier to *"eleven"* — which is, of course, much louder and *"better"* than *"ten."*

With Cruise, Towne, and action maestro Woo tapping a bottomless wellspring of studio dollars, *MI2* effortlessly outstrips the tired Bond film franchise, beating it at its own game. The film globe trots from Sydney, Australia to Moab, Utah, and on to Saville, Spain through the opening titles, dancing into a lively concoction of saucy double entendres, a worldly hero-heroine combo, a plethora of high-tech gadgetry, and a dastardly super-villain who holds the fate of the planet in his clutches.

The Hitchcock elements are overt, too: Hunt's superior (an uncredited cameo from Anthony Hopkins) orders him to seduce stunning super-thief Nyah Nordoff-Hall (Thandie Newton) into bedding her evil ex-beau Sean Ambrose (Dougray Scott) to get at the crucial plot 'MacGuffin' (Hitchcock's term for the catalytic plot device that is essentially unimportant to the audience). The MacGuffin here is a virulent super-virus code-named *"Chimera"* and its sole cure, *"Bellerophon,"* with which Ambrose courts amoral pharmaceutical mogul John McCloy (Brendan Gleeson of *The General*, 1998, *Lake Placid*, 1999, etc.) for big money and majority stock options in the firm. Ambrose indulges in a bit of intimate nastiness with his cigar-clipper and the finger-tip of his accomplice Hugh Stamp (Richard Roxburgh), and their discomforting chemistry recalls that between many a Hitchcock villain and confederate (i.e., James Mason and Martin Landau in *North by Northwest*, 1959, etc.).

So far, so good. Hunt's genuine heat (one refrains from calling anything in this vacuum love) for Hall makes him uncomfortable with her being a pawn: once Ambrose sees through Hall's false passion to divine her true mission, she is in mortal jeopardy. This is Hitchcock's *Notorious* (1946), plain and simple, with Cruise in the Cary Grant role, Newton a slinky substitute for Ingrid Bergman, and Scott filling Claude Rains' shoes while *"Chimera"* supplants that wine bottle filled with uranium. With Hunt's MI team in place — Luthor (Ving Rhames) returns to the series, joined by Aussie Billy Baird (John Polson) — the film glides into its best single sequence, a genuinely suspenseful racetrack encounter which skillfully synthesizes the various skills of the players, state-of-the-art gadgetry, and simmering interpersonal drama into a seamless whole. Woo handles this sequence with truly Hitchcockian precision; alas, it's all downhill from there.

In fact, the film begins its plunge down a slippery slope before the opening credits unreel. In the pre-credits sequence — when Ambrose doffs his impossibly-perfect 'Ethan Hunt' disguise in the pre-credits sequence, peeling it off like a mask in a Tex Avery cartoon — we know we are once more in a Hollywood CGI 'never-never' land. Such makeup trickery was crucial to the original *Mission: Impossible* TV series, wherein Martin Landau was the master of disguise using cutting-edge techniques to assume many roles. But Landau's meticulous applications, however extraordinary, were convincingly of this world — they took time to apply, relied on Landau's own chameleon vocal skills, and peeled off like real latex. *MI2*'s uncanny mask-and-wig combos and vocal patches (replicating any voice) are practically supernatural fabrications, applied and removed with an increasingly ridiculous instantaneousness that pushes *MI2* further into the realm of animated unreality, preparing the viewer for the cheats to come.

This is typical opportunistic 1990s short-term thinking. The cartoony CGI 'mask-off' effect briefly surprises us, but it also immediately undercuts the reportedly genuine stuntwork — Cruise climbing sheer cliff walls in Utah under the credits, his impressive gymnastics throughout — as seeing is no longer believing. Dig it: Jackie Chan's brand of stuntwork dazzles us because we accept it as real (as did the atheletic stuntwork of his precursors, from the silent era's Douglas

Fairbanks and Buster Keaton to 1970s icon Bruce Lee). We know that, however impossible such feats appear, Chan and his costars performed them at considerable risk to life and limb. This is what makes Chan's films so exhilarating to watch (the celebrated outtakes that accompany the closing credits of Chan's films reinforce their reality). But in *MI2* (as in so many modern Hollywood thrillers), however "real" the stuntwork, we cease to be amazed given the soup of CGI-enhanced nonreality they swim within. To paraphrase an old hippie joke, when there is no gravity, action films suck.

Amazement is vital to John Woo's movie-making; his flamboyant cinematic alchemy always hinged on gravity-defying feats and extravagant displays of gunplay and mayhem. When his seminal Hong Kong crime actioners trickled into the US a decade ago via the video bootleg market, Western audiences were dazzled by the intoxicating audacity of his work, which melded the brutal male-dominated cinema of Jean-Pierre Melville, Akira Kurosawa, Sergio Leone, and Sam Peckinpah with the dizzying kinetics of his native country's martial arts spectacles. *A Better Tomorrow* (*Ying Hung Boon Sik*, 1986), *A Better Tomorrow 2* (*Ying Hung Boon Sik II*, 1987), *The Killer* (*Dip Huet Seung Hung*, 1989), and *Hard-Boiled* (*Lat Sau San Taam*, 1992) indeed revolutionized international action cinema, justifiably rocketing both director Woo and their star, Chow Yun-Fat, into fresh opportunities.

Woo's films relied on reality-stretching stuntwork, grueling violence, and their lead characters' improbable capacity for absorbing massive quantities of lead, but these passionate 'bullet ballets' existed in their own convincing universe. Like the best horror films, they rigorously observed their own internal logic, however dreamlike the excesses. Excess – of emotion, suspended and extended motion, lead and bloodshed — was the route to sacred matyrdom, staged with a zeal that surpassed that characteristic of Kurosawa, Jean-Pierre Melville, Leone and Peckinpah. Chow Yun-Fat endured perforation by reality-defying quantities of bullets in the *Better Tomorrow* films and *The Killer*, but he still inevitably succumbed: the tragic finality of death could be delayed, but not avoided. The operatic enormity of his agonies elevated his suffering to transcendent religious extremes, evoking the most horrific agonies of the Christian saints, supplanting arrows with high-caliber bullets (churches, candles, white doves, and Madonnas reappear time and time again in Woo's Asian films, often amid gunplay). Woo's best Hong Kong features remain potent viewing experiences (as does Woo's most personal and intense film, *Bullet in the Head/Die Xue Jie Tou*, 1990), which can't be said for Woo's stateside films. *Broken Arrow* (1995) and *Face/Off* (1997) effectively showcased Woo's skills and obsessions (indeed, *Face/Off* is the best of all, truest to Woo's path), but *MI2* harks back to the ungainly compromises of his first US feature, the silly but entertaining Jean-Claude Van Damme vehicle *Hard Target* (1993).

Once Cruise climbs onto a motorcycle in *MI2*'s final act, the film slips into *Hard Target*'s hilarious Van Damme cycles-and-guns absurdities. By the time Cruise is skidding his feet on the tarmac at high speeds without shattering his ankles, shooting at gas caps instead of gas tanks to detonate spinning cars, leaping off his bike to collide with Ambrose in mid-air, and enduring ludicrous levels of punishment in the climax, the viewer is reduced to either helpless laughter or utter indifference. It's completely arbitrary which blow will finally put one of the antagonists down; we know they'll just pop up again like Tom and Jerry, or Itchy and Scratchy — and they do. Woo's style remains seductively kinetic and sensual, but *MI2* becomes a thriller that ceases to thrill. Woo is, pardon the pun, on Cruise-control here; despite the slow-mo flourishes, closeups of steely eyes, and images of cooing doves, nothing compares to the efficient craftsmanship of the comparatively tame racetrack sequence.

If you're a Cruise fan, you're going along for the ride regardless. For the rest of us, suffice to say if you're in the mood for *MI2*'s brand of cheeky, high-octane silliness, you'll have a ball — but if you're not, you'll just find it more exasperating, high-ticket Hollywood hogwash. *(Rated "PG-13" for language, partial nudity, adult and sexual situations, violence, gunplay, and "don't try this at home, kids" nonsense.)*

November 16:

Time to play a little catch-up this week. With this month claiming more hot new releases than any previous month in the history of home video (I kid you not), I'll make it quick and to the point this week. Here, in alphabetical order, are some of the top new releases waiting for you:

Martin Lawrence is a likable enough comedian, but he has yet to find a big-screen vehicle that lets him stretch. His early splash on TV and in the *House Party* films (1990-91) immediately thrust him into the Eddie Murphy flick *Boomerang* (1992), and it seems to have been a cat-and-mouse game between Lawrence and Murphy ever since. Lawrence has since climbed to co-star status with Murphy in the uneven Jim Crow-era prison pic *Life* (1999)[3]; every other Lawrence venture, it seems, simply drops him into Murphy's shadow. ***BIG MOMMA'S HOUSE*** (2000) is no exception, coming four years after Murphy's virtuoso turn playing the entire Klump family (under pounds of Rick Baker's state-of-the-art makeup work) in *The Nutty Professor* (1996), which leaned pretty heavily on tried-and-true 'fat and flatulence' jokes. *Big Momma's House* beat Murphy's *Nutty Professor* sequel *The Nutty Professor: The Klumps* (2000) into theaters by a week or two, and beats it again to the video shelves, but it'll be colder than a mackerel by the time Murphy reclaims his *Klump* crown next month. Playing an undercover FBI agent who happens to be a *"master of disguise,"* Lawrence cops just one of Murphy's Klump family members — revamped into the titular 'Big Momma' — and it's all he can do to keep this wheezing scatological comedy on its feet (or both cheeks, at least). Good for a few quick, cheap chuckles, but little else. *(Rated 'PG-13' for sexual innuendoes, gross-out humor, strong language, adult and sexual situations, and cops-and-killers violence.)*

BOYS AND GIRLS (2000) convinces me that Freddie Prinze, Jr. needs to either grow a brain or get a new agent. It's yet another variation on the Prinze, Jr. *"will he commit or not"* romantic drivel we've had more than enough of with ever-diminishing rewards (*She's All That*, 1999, *Down to You*, 2000). Commit to a good script, Freddie, please. This time he's an UC Berkeley engineering student hemming and hawing over free spirit Claire Forlani, and — oh, who cares. If you want to take the plunge, go for it, but the minute you pop that

---

[3] See *Blur, Vol. 1*, pp. 75-76.

tape in the VCR, you're being more decisive than Prinze's shallow preppie pinhead. Don't say I didn't warn you. *(Rated 'PG-13' for the usual coy 'adult' and sexual situations, language.)*

DEMENTIA (1953) is the latest, fascinating revival from the good folks at Kino Video, resurrecting John J. Parker's sole feature film, an overtly Freudian portrait of a disturbed young woman (Adrienne Barrett) lashing out at the male lechery that awaits her in every darkened alley, open doorway, and terrifying memory. Not for all tastes, *Dementia* is a weird, introspective fusion of 1940s film noir and the 1950s beat scene, of the American underground film movement (particularly the West Coast dreamlike 'psychodramas' of Maya Deren, Kenneth Anger, and Curtis Harrington) and the 1950s grindhouse exploitation circuit (co-directed by its lead male lech, Bruno Ve Sota, who soon became a fixture of Roger Corman drive-in horror films). To sweeten the pot for cinema lovers, the Venice California locals were later used by none other than Orson Welles to create the seedy border town of Los Robles in *Touch of Evil* (1958).

Filmed silent and unreeling without a single line of dialogue, *Dementia* boasts rich, expressionistic cinematography and a delirious musical score by George Antheil and soprano vocals by Marni Nixon (who provided the singing voices for Natalie Wood in *West Side Story*, 1961, and Deborah Kerr in *The King & I*, 1956). Upon completion, *Dementia* was rejected by the New York Censor Board, who demanded no less than sixteen cuts and reviled the film as *"indecent, inhuman... the quintessence of gruesomeness... overflows with horror, hope-*

lessness, strong sadism, violent acts of terror, and outbursts of panic." Ah, my kind of movie!

Parker abandoned his brainchild, and it remained shelved until film historian Herman G. Weinberg negotiated with the censors (who then agreed to only six cuts) for an 'adults only' urban art-house release of the film. Two years later, it resurfaced on the exploitation circuit as *Daughter of Horror* with a superfluous narration track by none other than Ed McMahon (yes, Johnny Carson's sidekick!), and popped up as the movie onscreen in *The Blob* (1958) when the protoplasmic monster threatened a downtown theater. Kino, bless 'em, offer both the restored *Dementia* and *Daughter of Horror* on their sterling video and DVD presentations, an alternative pick-of-the-week for cinephiles and adventurous viewers seeking livelier diversions than contemporary Hollywood can manage. *(Unrated; though tame by contemporary standards,* Dementia *still offers a few startling shocks involving a severed hand.)*

GOSSIP (2000) clicks instantaneously into the mean-spirit groove of *Cruel Intentions* (1999). A clique of college journalism students (James Marsden, Lena Headey, and Norman Reedus) concoct a malicious lie about fellow students Joshua Jackson and Kate Hudson just to see how far things will go. Things go, of course, completely out of control, and the malice behind their 'harmless' gossip bares its teeth as the truth behind Marsden's prior high school relations with rumor-victim Hudson emerges.

Flirting with volatile themes of campus sexual harassment and the extremes of *"date rape,"* Gossip steeps an attractive cast in its ugly emotional bile with decidedly mixed results. It will tantalize those predisposed to such cut-throat soap-operatics, and bore those who see through its thin tangle of narrative deceits, twists, and chicanery by the end of the first act. My teenagers and I were ready to toss our popcorn at the screen before the final contrived turn of the blade. Eric Bogosian adds a dash of venom as the smug journalism professor. *(Rated 'R' for strong language, adult and sexual situations, casual drug and alcohol use and abuse, and violence.)*

THE PERFECT STORM (2000) kicked up its own waves this summer. I noticed an interesting audience split on this major studio release: viewers under a certain age (say, early 20s) hated it, while older viewers (like myself) loved it. No joke, I think the problem is teenagers and younger adults simply can't relate to anyone laying their *lives* on the line for a job — while those of us who "know better" can't help but relate to the situation and its dire, seemingly inevitable consequences. (Who's the wiser? This schism may not be reflective of callow youthful indifference, as it is symptomatic of corporate American culture instilling at a tender age the pragmatic understanding that we are all expendable in the job market — so why make such an irrational investment/commitment? OK, back to the video review--)

Transplant German director-gone-Hollywood Wolfgang Peterson (*Das Boot*, 1981, *In the Line of Fire*, 1993, *Air Force One*, 1997) orchestrates a strong cast, polished production, and rousing special effects for this carefully-mounted condensation of Sebastian Junger's best-selling novel, based on the all-too-real Atlantic 'perfect storm' of October 1991 that claimed the lives of Gloucester, Massachusetts fishermen and others. I should also note that fans of the novel were sometimes disappointed; even at 130 minutes, the film cannot hold a candle to the depth, intensity, and wider canvas the novel form indulges. This fictionalized account crosscuts between a wide cast of characters, but its primary focus on down-on-his-luck and hungry-to-score Captain Billy Tyne (George Clooney) and his five-man crew (Mark Wahlberg, John C. Reilly, John Hawkes, William Fichtner, and Allen Payne) is rigorously maintained, building to its harrowing final act as they are caught in the belly of the raging beast.

Thankfully, the characters do *not* take a back seat to the impressive effects showcase, and that is the film's greatest accomplishment. Diane Lane delivers the strongest performance as Wahlberg's fiancee Christina, fearing the worst at home; it's another strong, understated role (on the heels of her turn in the excellent *My Dog Skip*[4]) that lends heart to the literal blood and thunder pounding around her. You'll never take a swordfish steak for granted again. Recommended! *(Rated 'PG-13' for language, brief sexual situations, casual alcohol abuse, the occupational hazards of fishing, and the violent intensity of the storm.)*

Informed and discriminating renters, please note: the release of *Hamlet* starring Ethan Hawke and Julia Stiles, originally announced for this week, has been postponed until 2001.[5]

---

[4] See *Blur, Vol. 2*, pp. 144-146.
[5] The November 16, 2000 *Brattleboro Reformer A&E* section also featured my article *"DeWees to Make Local Appearance,"* an overview of Vermont actor Rusty DeWees's career and his videos *The Logger* and *The Logger 2*. This article was revised, expanded, and published as *"Loving the Logger"* in *Green Mountain Cinema 1* (Black Coat Press, 2004).

November 23:

There's an eye-catching batch of animated features on the new release wall. One of the best of the new crop — the Dreamworks/Aardman Animation masterpiece *Chicken Run* — just hit stores two days ago, providing the ideal opportunity for a Thanksgiving holiday roundup of 'the Good, the Bad, and the Ugly' in this year's bumper crop.

Anyone who still considers such fare *"kid's stuff"* is cheating themselves out of a couple of the year's absolute best in any genre — it's your loss if you pass them up. Besides, you should all be aware by now that most of today's action and sf films are essentially CGI-animation features; just because they're plopping live-action stars like Tom Cruise in 'em doesn't mean you are not watching a cartoon.

Note that all actor's names listed this week are vocal performers, lending their voices to their respective clay, computer-generated, and/or cel-animated characters. I'll write up *Titan A.E.* and *Heavy Metal 2000* next week, and I heartily recommend *The Iron Giant* and *Princess Mononoke* [6] (which rank right up there with *Toy Story 2* and *Chicken Run*); there just wasn't space this week. Here's the rundown, in my own order of preference:

TOY STORY 2 (1999) is the best of the bunch, though *Chicken Run* (see below) is almost its equal. Dis-

---

[6] See *Blur, Vol. 1*, pp. 127-129, 211, 214, 217-218, and *Blur, Vol. 2*, pp. 181-187.

ney's corporate acquisition and nurturing of the cutting-edge computer-animation studio Pixar (*Toy Story*, 1995, *A Bug's Life*, 1998) is one of their smartest moves in the past decade. The Pixar artists are not only brilliant technicians and innovative pioneers, they are among the finest storytellers in America, period. *Toy Story 2* proves that directors John Lasseter, Lee Unkrich, and Ash Brannon can dance circles around most live-action filmmakers.

When a minor tear relegates Woody (Tom Hanks) to the shelf while "his boy" Andy takes off for summer cowboy camp, Woody's valiant rescue of another damaged toy from a yard sale places Woody in the selfish clutches of opportunistic toy collector Al McWhiggin (Wayne Knight). As Buzz Lightyear (Tim Allen) mounts a rescue mission to bring Woody back home before Andy's return, Al repairs Woody and adds him to his priceless collection of restored *"Woody's Roundup"* toys: Jessie the Cowgirl (Joan Cusack), Bullseye the Horse, and scheming Stinky Pete the Prospector (Kelsey Grammer), who look forward to their new life as museum pieces. Director Lasseter and his creative collaborators keep the pace brisk and breezy, building to a breathless conclusion that will have you in stitches.

Toy Story 2 juggles the playful and profound with high spirits and razor-sharp wit, timing, and characterizations. With Pixar's usual insouciant vigor, the gags fly fast and furious, with some of the best clearly targeting older viewers and movie-buffs (i.e., the character of *"The Cleaner"* is a sly reference to Luc Besson's 1990 *La Femme Nikita*; Wallace Shawn's lovable Rex is the running-*T. rex*-in-the-rear-view-mirror in a *Jurassic Park* gag; Buzz and the villainous Emperor Zug's revelation goofs on *Star Wars*, etc.). But *Toy Story 2* pointedly deals with its share of weighty human issues — abandonment, mortality, love, loyalty, rejection — without missing a beat. The film bears its heart during Jessie the Cowgirl's reverie, accompanied by Randy Newman's tune *"When She Loved Me"* (sung by Sarah McLachlan). It's simple, lyrical, and moving, an elegant *"less is more"* synthesis of music, song, and drama the Disney empire shouldn't forget in their rush to crank out more overblown animated musical extravaganzas. This is a magnificent film by any standard, not to be missed. *(Rated "G", suitable for all ages.)*

CHICKEN RUN (2000), the debut feature from Nick Parks and Peter Lord, the clay animation geniuses at the British Aardman Animation studios, is a marvelous entertainment and an ideal holiday season rental. Parks and Lord make the stretch to the necessities of the feature film format without losing one iota of the warmth, wit, and excitement of their justifiably celebrated *Wallace & Gromit* trio of animated short films (among other Aardman masterpieces like the memorable *Creature Comforts*, 1989 [7]).

One warning — and I'm dead serious about this — be sure to watch this absurdist epic *after* you've dined on your Thanksgiving turkey, lest you (and most of all the youngsters) lose any and all appetite for tender birdflesh.

Ah, but that's the point of *Chicken Run*, which anthropomorphizes the feathered denizens of Tweedy's Egg Farm who populate its brilliantly subversive synthesis of military 'escape' classics like *The Great Escape*

---

[7] Which gained a strong enough audience as a short film to manifest *two* TV series (2003, 2007).

(1963), *Stalag 17* (1953), *Flight of the Phoenix* (1965), and *The Bridge on the River Kwai* (1957). Under the tyrannical watch of greedy proprietor Mrs. Tweedy (Miranda Richardson) and her dim-witted husband (Tony Haygarth), the hapless hens plot a series of botched escape attempts led by dreamer Ginger (Julia Sawalha). While the rest of the roost resign themselves to the numbered-days of captivity, forced egg productivity, and the inevitable chopping block, Ginger's dream grows wings with the unexpected intrusion of a worldly rooster named Rocky (Mel Gibson), who promises to teach them all to fly once his wing heals. Rocky is, of course, a deceitful rascal, but the combination of Ginger's unflagging determination and the imminent threat of the Tweedy's latest get-rich-quick scheme (liquidating the egg farm to launch an automated chicken pie factory) leads to a wild and woolly climax.

The Aardman trademarks — beguiling characters, crisp staging and ever-inventive direction, satiric spins on tried-and-true plot devices, and hilarious Rube Goldberg gags and mechanical contraptions — are in full flower here. Highly Recommended! *(Rated "G", suitable for all ages, though younger viewers may find the unavoidable issue of chickens-as-food suitably disturbing.)*

FANTASIA 2000 (indeed released in 2000) has been squeezed onto the home video format less than a year after its limited-engagement as the first animated IMAX theatrical feature. It is as uneven an accomplishment and entertainment as its inspiration, the original *Fantasia* (1940). The animation showcased is lovely, sparkling with CGI enhancements and elements unimaginable by the original *Fantasia* animators, but whereas the original conception was ambitious and adventurous, the conception here is flawed. Despite its millennial title, the utterly conservative, derivative Disney orientation of *Fantasia 2000* undermines its implicit promise.

Take, for example, the musical selections that form the basis of the film, still rooted in the classical tradition with the sole exception of George Gershwin's *"Rhapsody in Blue."* Gershwin is the sole 20th Century American composer on tap; there's no Aaron Copeland, much less Frank Zappa or Windham Hill, in earshot. No surprise, either, that *"Rhapsody in Blue"* is the anthology's highlight, helmed by animation director Eric Goldberg as an independent short subject apart from the original *Fantasia 2000* project until the studio woke up to its potential. Elaborating on designs by celebrated cartoonist Al Hirschfeld (though much of the finished animation is closer to the fluid style of *New Yorker* cartoonist George Price), *"Rhapsody in Blue"* offers a lively day-in-the-life portrait of the Big Apple, and it is by far *Fantasia 2000*'s finest entry. Eric Goldberg also helms the film's other highlight, a two-and-a-half minute slapstick confection timed to Camille Saint-Saens' *"Carnival of the Animals, Finale"* [8] involving a lone anarchist flamingo with a yo-yo wreaking havoc amid a flock rank-and-file conformists; it's hilarious, and an apt metaphor for the breathe of fresh air director Goldberg's antics provide amid the stodgy Disney perfectionism.

Fantasia 2000 opens with the same flawed illogic of the original, pitching Beethoven's *"Symphony No. 5"*

---

[8] Note that Chuck Jones used this same piece of music, married to Warner Bros. animation, for a TV special back in the 1970s.

as a backdrop for animated geometric abstractions that all-too-soon coalesce into anthropomorphized butterflies, immediately establishing the studio's inherent distrust of pure, non-representational animation (as practiced by pioneers of the form like Len Lye and Norman McClaren). They also trot out Mickey Mouse's classic 1940 *Fantasia* turn as *"The Sorcerer's Apprentice,"* which still enchants as it shows up the paucity of imagination surrounding it. Ottorino Respighi's *"Pines of Rome"* inspires a lavish but vapid setpiece about an infant whale separated from its airborne parents amid an arctic landscape; Shostakovich's *"Piano Concerto No. 2, Allegro, Opus 102"* accompanies a tedious CGI revamp of Hans Christian Anderson's *"The Steadfast Tin Soldier,"* laundered into a melodrama in which the one-legged soldier rescues the petite ballerina from a lecherous Jack-in-the-Box. Sir Edgar Elgar's pompous *"Pomp and Circumstance"* will drive any high-school graduate from the room despite the silly Donald-Duck-on-Noah's-Ark cartoon affixed to it. In conclusion, Igor Stravinsky's *"Firebird Suite"* fuels *"a mythical story of life, death, and renewal"* (so says Angela Lansbury in the segment's intro) that shamelessly lifts and revamps imagery and narrative elements from Hayao Miyazaki's *Princess Mononoke* (1997, US release 1999), dividing that great film's mystical 'forest god' into an elemental trinity of male Elk, female forest sprite, and demonic Firebird. (Do yourself a favor and see *Princess Mononoke* instead.) [9]

Though it contains much eye and ear candy to savor, *Fantasia 2000* is, at best, an engaging failure. The vivid DVD release adds luster and a great many extras to

---

[9] See *Blur, Vol. 2*, pp. 181-187.

its presentation, including audio commentaries by executive producer Roy E. Disney, conductor James Levine, and producer Don Ernst, as well as the directors and arti directors of each segment; two 1953 musical cartoon shorts (the abrasive *Adventures in Music: Melody* and livelier Academy-Award winner *Toot, Whistle, Plunk, and Boom*); a commemorative booklet, and much more. The true bounty, however, is to be had in the box set called *The Fantasia Anthology*, which includes Disney's extras-laden DVDs of both *Fantasia* and *Fantasia 2000*, with an exclusive third disc, *The Fantasia Legacy: Fantasia Continued*, a 48-minute compilation of production interviews, deleted scenes, abandoned concepts, and publicity materials for the millennial release. Particularly amusing is the spectacle of various straight-arrow Disney mouthpieces skirting the fact that *Fantasia*'s 1969-1970 revival and popular reassessment was due in large part to the patronage of a wide-eyed, dope-smoking counterculture which embraced the film's re-release as an ideal extension of *2001: A Space Odyssey*'s mind-bending *"ultimate trip."* [10] *(Rated "G", suitable for all ages.)* [11]

---

[10] When I first saw *Fantasia* in a theater, it was in a downtown Burlington, VT theater – the Strong or the Flynn — during the 1969 rerelease. I went with my mother, Anita, who had fond memories of seeing the film during its original release – and she wondered aloud what that smell *"like burning rope"* was that greeted us as soon as we entered the theater! Sweet.

[11] This review was also published in *The Video Watchdog* #72, June 2001, pp. 10-11; as noted in the book introduction, all reviews also published in *VW* are archived here with the complete 'best text' synthesis of both the newspaper and the *VW* edits, and should be considered the definitive final edit.

POKEMON 2000: THE POWER OF ONE (*Gekijô-Ban Poketto Monsutâ: Maboroshi no Pokemon: Rugia Bakutan*, 2000) is about — ah, ah, *ah* — *YAAAAAAAAA! POKEMON! Six new characters! WAAAAUUUGH!* Multiple plot threads scattered like a rabid dog's scat! *Ya-Ya-Ya-YAAAAAAAAAAA!* Ash Ketchum and Pikachu in trouble when the weather heads south (like, way south) on Shamouti Island!! *Team Rocket to the rescue!!! Bad collector Lawrence III wants Moltres, Articuno, Zapdos, and, and, and—- ah, ah, ah-Ya-YYYYAAAAAAAGHHHH!* The Legendary Lugia is coming – no, wait, wait, *wait — aaaaaaaaaaaaYa-Ya-Ya- YAAAAAAGGGGGHH!*

This cacophony of color, movement, and *really* high-pitched voices and music will delight the devoted *Pokemon* fans and card collectors, and the film is savvy enough to aim a few barbs at its own shameless hucksterism and the whole *Pokemon* card madness. All others beware.

The opening short film, *Pikachu's Rescue Adventure* (*Poketto Monsutâ: Pikachû Tankentai*, 2000), is almost as hallucinogenic as *Pikachu's Vacation* (*Poketto Monsutâ: Pikachû no Fuyu-Yasumi*, 1999), which accompanied the first feature,[12] but it eases along at a much more measured pace, lulling unsuspecting parents and at-risk heart-patient grandparents into thinking their tickers might make it through the feature. It's not for you and I, Bunky. *(Rated "G", suitable for all ages.)*

---

[12] See *Blur, Vol. 1*, pp. 210-218, 238-241.

November 30:

GLADIATOR (2000) is the talk of the town this week, thanks to its video debut. Working as I do in a video store, part of the fun is listening to (and exchanging) views on new movies in theaters and on the racks. The diversity of opinions and the passion with which they are argued is remarkable; that is, after all, part and parcel of why movies are such a pleasure, as entertainments and as an artform. M. Night Shyamalan's *Unbreakable* is now in theaters and currently eliciting such polarizing arguments, and earlier this year *Gladiator* did the same while it graced the big screen. Folks either loved or hated the film, and I'm going to address some of those arguments here. (I hope one and all reading my weekly ramblings do so understanding that I'm just offering my two-cents worth, and hopefully I don't abuse the privilege of the podium too much.)

In short, *Gladiator* is an epic melodrama, true to the classic Italian tradition initiated in the silent era and quickly adopted by Hollywood before the coming of sound. The respective spectacles of Roman or Greek pageantry, excess, corruption and retribution, mad tyrants, senatorial intrigue, and the ever-intoxicating allure and atrocities of war and the arena have remained fixtures of the genre from the multiple novel adaptations of *Ben-Hur* (1907, 1925, 1959) to *The Last Days of Pompeii* (1900, 1908, 1913, 1926, 1935, 1940, 1950, 1959, 1975) to the beefcake *"sword-and-sandal"* entries of the 1950s and '60s (the Italians called them *'peplum,'* plural form *'pepla,'* referring to the toga costuming such films rely upon). Ridley Scott's *Gladiator* is the latest spin on this venerable archetype, and it's a properly clanging, noisy, bloody, and rousing piece of work.

Taken on its own terms — a revamp of the genre for the new Millennium, by way of Kirk Douglas and Stanley Kubrick's *Spartacus* (1960) — *Gladiator* is a marvelous adventure film, applying all the contemporary state-of-the-art CGI effects (short for Computer-Generated Imagery, you'll recall; I'll be belaboring the acronym terribly this week) available to the task. Thus, Rome in all its glory is rendered on a scope and scale prior generations of filmmakers could only dream of, and Scott (director of *The Duelists*, 1977, *Alien*, 1979, *Blade Runner*, 1982, *Thelma & Louise*, 1991, etc.) is just the man to embrace both the technology and genre with unabashed zeal.

Gladiator is further graced with a genuinely stellar performance from extraordinary Australian actor Russell Crow, who inhabits his role of Spanish-born General Maximus with the same physical and emotional conviction he brought to everything from *Romper Stomper* (1992, as a reckless proto-Nazi skinhead) to *The Insider* (1999, as middle-aged, put-upon tobacco-industry whistle-blower Jeffrey Wigand).[13] Crowe is a chameleon who works from the inside out, and he breathes uncanny life into the entirety of the film by so perfectly embodying all that Maximus is and aspires to: brave soldier, devoted father and husband, betrayed veteran, and lethal gladiator seeking retribution, freedom, and deliverance. Director Scott, his creative and technical collaborators, and the supporting cast (including Joaquin Phoenix, Connie Nielsen, and wizened British vets Richard Harris and — in his final triumphal role — Oliver Reed) match Crowe with their best efforts, too, but make no mistake: Crowe

---

[13] See *Blur Vol. 2*, pp. 34-37.

makes *Gladiator*'s oft-creaking claptrap work like a charm.

Having successfully expanded the parameters of Rome and his lord Caesar Marcus Aurelius (Harris) with a decisive confrontation with the Germanic hordes, Maximus' desire to return to home and hearth are thwarted by cut-throat Caesar heir-apparent Commodus (Phoenix), who (living down to his name's implicit kinship to a bathroom fixture) opportunistically slays his father and betrays Maximus by ordering the execution of the general and his family. Maximus survives, his family succumbs, and Maximus finds himself enslaved by gladiatorial circus entrepreneur Proximo (Reed), forced to fight in the arena for the entertainment of the masses. Seizing on the eventuality of confronting and possibly killing Commodus to avenge his family, Maximus excels at his new role amid an ever-escalating procession of arena horrors. Nothing new here, really, but Crowe makes us believe in Maximus; thus, we believe in his quest, and go for the ride. In an odd but vivid way, *Gladitator* also crystallizes our own current dissatisfaction with government and our own feelings of disenfranchisement, of being betrayed by our rulers; that, I suspect, accounts for its emotional resonance.

I, Claudius,[14] it isn't, and many viewers who didn't care for the film (including celebrity critics like Roger Ebert) criticized the usual genre staples: too much mayhem, erotic intrigue, distortions of historical facts, and a cast mouthing all manner of regional accents. *"This*

---

[14] This is a reference to the excellent 1976 BBC/London Film Productions miniseries, which I seemed to use as a yardstick a lot in *Video Views*, having just screened it in 1999 without an excuse to write about it in *Video Views*.

wasn't Rome," some of them said, and they're right. You want history? Read; big-budget films have never, ever been a source of reliable historical info. You want Rome? Learn Latin or get used to subtitles. You want an accurate portrait of the era? Let's face it, to our modern sensibilities, Rome would be an utterly repellent alien planet, leaving the delirious *Fellini Satyricon* (1969) as the 'truest' portrait we're capable of vicariously entering (or tolerating). Accents a problem? The genre has always indulged such a hodgepodge (including the dubbed *Hercules pepla*), in which British accents ring *"truer"* for many American audiences who could care less; even the extraordinary BBC serial *I, Claudius* (1976, available on DVD from Image Entertainment) suffered this problem; note the nod to *Claudius* with the sly casting of Derek Jacoby as a sympathetic senator. Yes, Commodus is a dim echo of the real corruption Rome's most terrifying despots personified; for that, the justifiably infamous X-rated Bob Guccione travesty *Caligula* (1980) and Joe D'Amato's even more depraved (!) knock-offs [15] come closest to the mark, and they *still* fall short of the genuine excesses history has recorded.

Gladiator at times strains and creaks. Despite his growing madness and the stacked-deck, it's hard to swallow Commodus actually entering an arena with Maximus for any reason, but such are the requirements

---

[15] Joe D'Amato was one of a multitude of pseudonames used by prolific Italian director Aristide Massaccesi (1936-1999), whose almost 200 films included *Caligula* rips *Caligola: La Storia mai Raccontata/Caligula: The Untold Story* (1982, under the name 'David Hills') and *Caligola: Follia del Potere/Caligula: The Deviant Emperor* (1995/97, as 'Raf De Palma' and 'Joe D'Amato').

of melodrama. We ache for the confrontation as much as Maximus does, and would turn our demanding thumbs down on anything less.

Gladiator is not for the impressionably young or squeamish. Scott stages the extended battle sequences with the quivering, gore-spattered 'you are there' immediacy of the opening D-Day horrors of Steve Spielberg's *Saving Private Ryan* (just as Oliver Stone extended the same techniques to the rousing football sequences of *Any Given Sunday*),[16] and that prompted some negative comments from customers. Its realism may be too much for some; but Scott's techniques work, and they owe an equal debt (as does Spielberg) to the remarkable battle sequences of Peter Watkins' BBC teleplays *Cullodon* (1964) and *The War Game* (1965) and Orson Welles' *Chimes at Midnight* (aka *Falstaff*, 1967). All in all, *Gladiator* is a vivid, sensual creation and a rousing entertainment, an often breathtaking epic that rigorously keeps its intimate focus on its lead characters. It may be old wine in a new bottle, but it's a pretty good vintage.

We recommend pouring it into a *wide* glass — via Universal/Dreamworks' 16:9 DVD, a deluxe twin-pack that comes proudly labeled as containing *four extra hours* of supplemental material. The first disc contains the feature, letterboxed at 2.35 with optional Dolby Digital or DTS 5.1 sound, with a commentary by Ridley Scott; the second contains HBO's *First Look* program devoted to the film, The Learning Channel's *The Bloodsport of a Gladiator*, 25m of deleted scenes (viewable with dialogue or Scott's commentary), a 7m montage of additional unused footage, an interview with composer Hans Zimmer, two 'making of' featurettes, the pages of

---

[16] See *Blur, Vol. 2*, pp. 178-180.

a production diary kept by young actor Spencer Treat Clark (who played Lucius, and co-stars in *Unbreakable*), conceptual art and storyboards, and an extensive photo gallery – all for just $10 more. Thumbs down on VHS.

The film itself, though, is most highly recommended! *(Rated "R" for violence, gore, adult and sexual situations.)* [17]

TITAN A.E. and ***HEAVY METAL 2000***: In this CGI-dominated era, many live-action films are essentially lavish animated features; *Gladiator* certainly is, with nary a shot that didn't require some CGI-enhancement, and the novel use of CGI to complete Oliver Reed's central role in the wake of the actor's unfortunate death during filming (furthering a technique that previously rescued 1994's *The Crow* from the tragic death of its star, Brandon Lee). Thus, animated features face a real dilemma in the age of live-action "cartoons" like *Mission Impossible 2* and *The X-Men* (which I'll be reviewing next week): unless animated features create a wholly fresh "new" reality, they fall short of the "anything goes" worlds CGI-enhanced live-action fantasies revel in. Thus, *Toy Story 2* and *Chicken Run* succeed, because they *do* create wholly-fresh animated realities we can fall into and enjoy; their respective worlds peopled with living toys and clay-animated anthropomorphised fowls are enticing and convincing on their own terms. Meanwhile, animated features that might have passed muster in the pre-CGI era of the 1970s and '80s by emulating live-action fantasies have become anachronisms. They fall short both as animated works (by not

---

[17] An adapted version of this review was also published in *The Video Watchdog* #70, April 2001, pp. 18-20.

creating their own unique universes) and as pastiches of live-action efforts.

Though they are very different films in many regards, both *Titan A.E.* (2000) and *Heavy Metal 2000* (filmed under the title *F.A.K.K. 2*, finished in 1999 though its cable debut was this past summer) are failures for the reasons I've just described. Both are derivative futuristic action-fantasies, lifting their thin plot lines from tried-(or tired)-and-true live-action science-fiction films (*Star Wars* above all — both plots are driven by the loss of a father, and pit their respective hero/heroine against dire extraterrestrial villains). Both films rely upon an uneasy blend of traditional cel animation and the new CGI animation techniques with variable results, never settling into a consistent look, texture, or convincingly whole imaginary universe; they are chaotic, crazy-quilt tapestries of sometimes incompatible visual styles and mismatched designs. Thus, neither successfully creates a seamless, convincing *"new reality"* unique to themselves. They are, in short, shadows of better films, and sadly, they were conceived as such.

That said, their differences are telling. Whereas *Heavy Metal 2000* is obsessed with revenge, *Titan A.E.* concerns itself with rebirth. *Titan A. E.* is the better of the two films; it's also the only one suitable for younger viewers (which lends *Heavy Metal 2000* a certain erotically-charged exoticism). Set in the 40th Century, *Titan A.E.* places the salvation of mankind quite literally in the palm of its young hero, Cale (voice by Matt Damon), as a map genetically-encoded into his hand is the key to the shambling storyline as the villainous Drej seek nothing less than the extermination of our species from the universe. Producer/directors Don Bluth[18] (*The Secret of NIMH*, 1982, *An American Tale*, 1986, *The Land Before Time*, 1988, etc.) and Gary Goldman manage to breathe some life into the story (co-scripted by *Buffy the Vampire Slayer* creator Joss Whedon), and orchestrate at least one bracing sequence set amid the *"Ice Rings of Tigrin"* in the *"Andali Nebula"* (like Tolkeinesque fantasies, such sf confections juggle as many exotic names and locals as possible). In an imaginative variation on the old submarine movie slide through mine-infested waters, the *"Ice Rings"* sequence turns into a frantic chase through ever-shifting-and-shattering monolithic ice crystals, and its one of the few passages that is both gripping and beautiful.

Heavy Metal 2000, on the other hand, is awash in violence, gore, rape, nudity, foul language, and inane dialogue. *Titan A.E.* has its share of corkers, too, but nothing to approach *"Hey, you, ugly — your mother's a Hectarian Whore's hand-bag." Heavy Metal 2000* is full of such plucky gems, with the vocal talents of Julie Strain-Eastman, Michael Ironside, and Billy Idol savoring every snarl and cussword for what little it's worth. The film is a sequel in name only to the erratic 1981 animated feature *Heavy Metal*, an 'R'-rated Canadian-produced anthology that buried one or two effective segments amid much substandard and sophomoric material. Withheld from legitimate release for almost two decades (reportedly due to soundtrack music rights), *Heavy Metal* gained the allure of 'forbidden fruit' on the bootleg video market, tantalizing too as one of the few successors to Ralph Bakshi's pioneer adult animations

---

[18] Note that *Titan A.E.* remains Bluth's final feature film to date.

(*Fritz the Cat*, 1972, *Heavy Traffic*, 1973, etc.). *Heavy Metal 2000* tentatively offers vestigial links to the original *Heavy Metal* feature: a buried extraterrestrial element causes catalytic transformations in both films, and a street flesh peddler in *HM 2000* resembles the villain of the original film's climactic episode, which likewise featured a female warrior cussing and cutting up.

Though producer Kevin Eastman (co-creator of *Teenage Mutant Ninja Turtles*) kept his name off the finished product (save for a *"based on"* credit), this was Kevin's show all the way, drawn from his ambitious graphic novel *Melting Pot* (1986-93, co-created with credited Simon Bisley and uncredited Eric Talbot). His Amazonian, 6' 1" wife is busy direct-to-video starlet Julie Strain (veteran of Andy Sidaris' actioners like *Fit to Kill*, 1993, and *L.E.T.H.A.L. Ladies: Return to Savage Beach*, 1998, along with other filmmakers' efforts like *Sorceress*, 1995, etc.), and she "stars" as the bloodthirsty 'F.A.K.K.2', lifting this unwieldy moniker from graffiti seen at the site of her father's death (defined in a throwaway line as *"Federation Assigned Ketogenic Killzone to the Second Level,"* meaning *"Death Planet"*). Kevin Eastman bought the New York-based adult comics magazine *Heavy Metal* about a decade ago, ultimately deciding the magazine's title was a far more marketable commodity (wed as it is to the 1981 film which recently enjoyed great success in the video market); under its original *F.A.K.K. 2* title, an embarrassingly crude novelization circulated in the late 1990s and the comics version of the film was showcased in the magazine's Summer, 1999 issue.

I wish I could champion the completed film, knowing how near and dear the project once was to Kevin's heart, and applaud his seeing it through sans studio support, but alas. To be blunt, like the original *Heavy Metal* movie, *HM 2000* simply isn't any good. It's crudely animated and revels in the same puerile fetishized obsessions that characterize the basest elements of *Heavy Metal* as a magazine (and the '81 movie). Sweat, swagger, breasts, blood, raging hormones, outsized weaponary, sexual insults and bullying banter can be entertaining, but *HM 2000* hasn't the wit, vigor, or audacity of a Bill Plympton, Russ Meyer, or even (sigh) Andy Sidaris. It's neither clever nor excessive enough to make anything of its relentless mayhem, and there's simply no life to it. It may please those seeking cheap thrills; all others, beware.

Titan A.E. and *Heavy Metal 2000* were ambitious undertakings, representative of the polar extremes of the current animation scene (the former made with millions of studio dollars, the latter an essentially self-financed low-budget effort). As such, they are interesting and at times entertaining diversions — but if you're seeking genuinely adult animation, see Hayao Miyazaki's *Princess Mononoke*... or, for that matter, the marvelous *Toy Story 2. (*Titan A.E. *is rated 'PG' for language and violence'* Heavy Metal 2000 *is rated "R" for violence, gore, strong language, nudity, rape, and sexual content.)*[19]

December 7:

With a flood of new releases in stores everywhere, it's time again for a quick-and-dirty rundown of the cur-

---

[19] The reviews (or abridgements) of *Heavy Metal 2000, Titan A.E.*, and *The X-Men* also appeared in *VMag* #37, January 2001, pp. 34, 36.

rent crop, all made in the year of our Lord, 2000 A.D.... though each and every one of them rely on source material from prior decades. Is it too much to ask that we get some fresh ideas on the cusp of the Millennium?

GONE IN 60 SECONDS is the latest amplified, adrenaline-pumped, mind-numbing Jerry Bruckheimer (*Armageddon*, 1998, *The Rock*, 1996, etc.) production, a nominal in-name-only remake of stunt man H.B. Halicki's 1974 drive-in classic. In the original, producer-director Halicki starred (and stunt-drove) as a car thief betrayed by his employer, prompting an extravagant police chase. Though crudely-made even by 1970s standards and muddled by a turgid first hour, Halicki scored a grass-roots box-office hit thanks to the climactic 42-minute (!!!) chase that gleefully totaled over 90 vehicles with style. Hey, top that, Bruckheimer! Well, he can't, and doesn't.

Instead, the new, "improved" *Gone in 60 Seconds* substitutes a wasted top-drawer cast (led by Nicolas Cage, Angelina Jolie, Giovanni Ribisi, and Delroy Lindo) orchestrating a super-heist (stealing 50 autos in 12 hours) amid episodic complications that builds to a flaccid 14-minute climactic chase capped by one of those stupid 1990s vehicular jumps we've all grown sooooo tired of seeing. Bad-movie mavens can revel in the absurdist clipped dialogue, eccentric characters, and occasional inadvertent laugh, but director Dominic Sena (who helmed the much better *Kalifornia* in 1993) mounts a lackluster effort. For all the talk of muscle cars and auto expertise, the camera never caresses the engines or machines; even the 'lead' vehicle, a Shelby Mustang GT 500 nicknamed 'Eleanor,' is reduced to a cipher. Heck, Sena doesn't even fetishize Jolie's pouty lips.

Halicki did it better in '74, squeezing far more bank-for-the-buck out of his 'Eleanor,' a virtually-indestructible 1973 Ford Mustang. The new *Gone in 60 Seconds* spent more on its title sequence than the original version cost in its entirety, but it doesn't hold a candle to Halicki's low-budget, gut-level redneck thrills. *(The original 1974* Gone in 60 Seconds *is suitable for all ages, peppered with some strong language; the new version is rated "R" for violence, language, nudity, and sexual situations.)*

THE NUTTY PROFESSOR II: THE KLUMPS proves once again how major studio feature films rarely serve our finest comedians. Eddie Murphy once electrified the screen, even when his vehicles (including the star-making *48 Hours* back in '82) were unworthy. His finest cinematic hour remains his first concert film *Eddie Murphy Raw* (1987), which amply showcased his greatest strengths (mimicry, sharp wit) and weaknesses (misogyny, a foul tongue sans the wicked intent his precursor Richard Pryor brought to wielding harsh language as a tool). After a decade-long career spiral, Murphy's inspired performance in the 1996 *The Nutty Professor* brought his chameleon-like abilities to the fore again (aided by makeup master Rick Baker's phenomenal work) and put the man back on top.

As shy, overweight, and utterly-likeable college professor Sherman Klump, Murphy did the unexpected and created a genuine character amid the sloppy slapstick revamp of Jerry Lewis' 1963 classic comedy spin on Robert Louis Stevenson's *Dr. Jekyll and Mr. Hyde*. As in the Lewis original, a chemical concoction doesn't create a shaggy monster, but a slim, suave, insensitive, lounge-lizard ladies' man named Buddy Love, Klump's alter-ego (a concept lifted, by the way, from not one but two British films that pre-dated Jerry Lewis's opus, *The Ugly Duckling,* 1959, and *The Two Faces of Dr. Jekyll* aka *House of Fright*, 1960, both from Hammer Films). The inevitable complications of romance and split-personality were peppered by Murphy's delightful multi-character role as Sherman's entire family, as foul-mouthed, flatulent, and raucous a family unit as an Eddie Murphy fan could wish for. A little of the Klumps went a long way, but Sherman remained the main attraction, lending the film spark and heart.

Well, the Klump clan is back in full force in this uninspired retread, which sadly pushes Sherman to the sidelines too often to make room for Murphy's virtuoso spin as Mama, Papa, Ernie, and Granny (and, of course, Buddy Love). Alas, more Klumps and less Sherman takes a toll, and spark and heart take a back seat to back-side jokes. The opening wedding sequence, as Sherman's worst fears about his affection for fiance Denise Gaines (Janet Jackson) erupt on the alter, promptly asserts the sexual and scatological orientation of the rest of the film. Worse yet, the ramshackle screenplay (by five writers, no less) top-loads the narrative with all sorts of nonsense: Sherman's youth-formula prompts corporate espionage; Sherman hides it in the Klump refrigerator, where it fires the clan libido; Sherman purges Buddy Love from his own genetic code, but suffers increasing loss of intelligence as a result; Buddy Love's resurrection relies on a canine hair as a catalytic agent, prompting Love to opportunistically demonstrate dog-behavior whenever laughs lag.

There are moments — funny one-liners and bits, a tidy little *Armageddon* and *Star Wars* parody, amusing outtakes under the final credits — and vet character actress Kathleen Freeman (from vintage Jerry Lewis films like the original *Nutty Professor*) scores a smile with her uncredited cameo, still a sassy comedienne at age 81. Amid it all, Murphy (again collaborating with Rick Baker's remarkable makeup creations) gives his all to ever-diminishing returns. Murphy doesn't stint, but the laughs are fewer and further between, proof once again that less is more — and more is much, much less when it comes to overblown, overproduced, over-calculated filmmaking-by-committee sequels. Feed 'em all to the giant hamster, I say. *(Rated "PG-13" for really strong language, abundance of sexist and fat jokes, juvenile takes on adult situations, sexual innuendo, nudity, and violence.)*

OCTOPUS is a US-Russian coproduction, which bodes well for future relations between the superpowers, demonstrating open policies concerning once top-secret documents and proving that the world 'round, a singularly stupid monster movie is a universal commodity. Top-secret info: Did you know that during the 1962 Cuban missile crisis, U.S. torpedoes sank a Russian sub carrying biological warfare weaponry to Castro? No? Did you know that 35 years later, that biological hazard created a jumbo mutant sub-sucking octopus with anemia and nasty mouthparts unlike any cephalopod known to mankind (outside of the slick but stupid 1998 monster movie *Deep Rising*, which this mini-epic emulates)?

Ol' eight-arms tanks a U.S. nuclear sub and tackles a luxury liner, stranding the sub on the ocean floor for almost half the film's running time where even minimal logic (the effects of deep-sea pressure and water intake, etc.) erodes until the final shot. For instance: after the sub survives a tussle with the monster, smashing control-room equipment and hurling sailors about like rag dolls, a shot of the cabin belonging to the female cephalopod expert on board (the truly wretched Carolyn Lowery) opens with unbroken glass test-tubes and beakers all in place on a table top. There's bogus action and espionage (the latter dished out by villainous Ravil Isyanov, the only cast member who can act) and acceptable CGI monster effects by London-based Magic Camera Company Limited. It's all derivative of Ray Harryhausen's *It Came From Beneath the Sea* (1955), which still tops this clunker, the first and worst of many direct-to-video giant-animal pics of the winter (next: *Crocodile, Spiders*, and *Python!*), most of which were brain-stormed by *Octopus*'s story author Boaz Davidson. *"Battle stations! Dive! Dive!" (Rated "PG-13" for language, violence, and Lowery's wet t-shirt.)*

THE REPLACEMENTS: Gene Hackman as coach Jimmy McGinty lends a little anchor and Keanu Reeves lends his good looks to this lightweight football comedy. Actually, Reeves (now 35 years old, believe it or not) plays straight-man to the rest of the team as has-been quarterback Shane Falco, whose reputation for fumbling in the final clinch haunts his every waking moment. McGinty gives Falco and a pack of talented misfits a second chance at glory when a team strike... oh, does it really matter what the plot is? The cast is fun: Jon Favreau (*Swingers*, 1996, *Very Bad Things*, 1998, etc.) is psycho Danny Bateman (get it? Bateman? As in *American Psycho*?), Brooke Langton (also of *Swingers*) provides the romantic entanglements as cheerleader-leader Annabelle Farrell; Orlando Jones (7-Up's latest commercial sweep lead) is the cowardly, loud-mouthed runner; Rhys Ifans (*Notting Hill*, 1999) is the cocky Welsh soccer star in place as knock-out kicker; vet character actor Jack Warden is the feisty, corrupt team owner; underrated Gailard Sartain (of Ernest fame and countless supporting roles) is assistant coach Leo Pilachowski; and sportscasters John Madden and Pat Summerall guy themselves.

Locker-room cliches dominate, from the embarrassing team dance-number to Gloria Gaynor's *"I Will Survive,"* to Reeves and Langton play their love scene to play-by-play sportscaster commentary. John Hughes acolyte Howard Deutch directs; Deutch previously helmed *Pretty in Pink* (1986), *Some Kind of Wonderful* (1987), and more recently *Grumpier Old Men* (1995) and *The Odd Couple II* (1998), and he lends *The Replacements* his usual shallow, efficient, crowd-pleasing manner. It's all candy, and goes down without a toothache. *(Rated "PG-13" for strong language, football action and violence played for laughs, and adult and sexual content primarily involving the cheerleaders, two of whom are erotic dancers.)*

The miracle of the film version of **THE X-MEN** is that it makes any coherent sense whatsoever. It's based on the popular and utterly interminable Marvel mutant soap-opera comicbook series which debuted in 1963. But, lo and behold, skilled director (and obvious *X-Men* comic-book fan) Bryan Singer (*The Usual Suspects*, 1995) lovingly plucks the cherries from writer Chris Claremont's tenure on the comic series, mobilizing a stellar cast and cutting-edge CGI wizardry to craft a crackling, concise, and surprisingly effective sf-fantasy potboiler that ranks among the best of its genre.

Singer immediately hits the proper tone with three bold narrative strokes: opening the film with a flashback to the Nazi concentration camp trauma that reveals the powers, and hard-earned distrust of humanity, fueling the adult crusade of nominal villain Magneto (Ian McKellen); teenager Rogue (Anna Paquin) suffering her own intimate trauma in a pubescent bedroom encounter that unveils her latent mutant powers and sends her fleeing from her home life; and a provocative United Nations encounter between lecturing scientist/mutant Dr. Jean Gray (Famke Janssen) and hate-monger Senator Kelly (Bruce Davison), fomenting his crusade against mutants that provokes the first onscreen confrontation between Magneto and the benevolent Professor Charles Xavier (Patrick Stewart in a role he was born for). Singer thus establishes the ambitious historical and international scope of the narrative while tapping the volatile teenage core audience of the comic and movie. Rogue's situation succinctly embodies the confusion of feeling like an outsider while longing for acceptance, found in a fringe group of fellow 'freaks,' herein real mutants; the tangle of self-loathing and empowerment linked with one's budding sexuality.

Few literary adaptations, much less comic-book adaptations, are so perfectly in tune with their source material, and sure-footed in their translation of their chosen source's core elements to film (for the record, the incarnation of the venerable mutant team the film adapts dates from the 1970s onward, launched in *The Uncanny X-Men* #94 by comics scripter Len Wein and artist Dave Cockrum, thereafter helmed by writer Chris Claremont working with artist John Byrne, among many others). Singer doesn't miss a step, escalating from the Canadian pit-fight bar meeting of Rogue and Wolverine (Hugh Jackman) to the climactic struggle against Magneto and his minions atop the Statue of Liberty with high energy and narrative precision.

The X-Men and their opponents are a winning mutant menagerie, with the chemistry between Wolverine and Rogue providing heart, the ire between Wolverine and Cyclops (James Marsden) simmering throughout to great effect, and the blue-skinned shape-shifter Mystique (Rebecca Romjin-Stamos) lending a truly scary, mercurial presence to the proceedings. A pleasant surprise, all in all, bringing formidable intelligence to its alternative fantasy-world and occasionally silly genre archetypes; well worth a look, even if you *think* you won't like it. *(Rated "PG-13" for language, super-hero violence, and some adult situations handled with taste and discretion.)*

December 14:

PICK OF THE WEEK: The five-tape video set (or four-disc, on DVD) showcasing the entire first season of the celebrated HBO series ***The Sopranos*** (1999), created and supervised by writer-director David Chase. Though a veteran of TV series like *Northern Exposure* (1993-95), *The Rockford Files* (1976-80), and *I'll Fly Away* (1992-93),[20] by Chase's own admission *The Sopranos* represents his first chance to really strut his stuff, sans the restrictions of network-television standards & practices and the strait-jacket of commercials (which by their very nature disrupt dramatic pacing, increasingly curtail running times, and require the breakdown of a program

---

[20] Fellow horror movie fans, note: David Chase's first screenwriting credits were for the sleeper *Grave of the Vampire* (1974) and as story consultant for *Kolchak: The Night Stalker* (1974-75), for which he scripted eight episodes.

into four acts, however arbitrary or false that structure may end up being). The result is remarkable. Those of us lacking access to HBO can finally see for ourselves what the brouhaha was all about — and we don't have to wait a week or more for the next episode. *The Sopranos* is that rarity, a TV event that lives up to the praise and attendant buzz. It's all here: thirteen one-hour episodes, plus extras (the DVD set offers over fifteen hours of viewing, including Chase's director commentary for the debut installment and a one hour, 17 minute interview moderated by vet film director Peter Bogdanovich). It's well worth the effort.

The Sopranos chronicles, with intimate detail, the day-to-day challenges faced by 'waste management consultant' Tony Soprano (James Gandolfini), a New Jersey mobster who is forced to seek therapy after he suffers a series of 'blackouts' triggered by family-related crisis. The conundrum here (and source of much of the series' pitch-black humor) is Tony's ongoing ability to deal with the brutality of his profession, and his inability to cope with matters of the heart: when an adopted family of ducks literally fly the coop, Tony's down for the count; when his dour mother Livia (the late Nancy Marchand, who died after completing the first two seasons) expresses her extreme dissatisfaction with the nursing home they're visiting, Tony collapses. Enter therapist Dr. Jennifer Melfi (Lorraine Bracco of *Goodfellas*), who Tony visits in strictest secrecy, knowing if word gets out he's seeing a counselor, fears over what Tony may or may not be talking about could attract unwanted (and most likely lethal) attention.

Similar scenarios have already been grist for comedies like *National Lampoon's The Don's Analyst* (1997) and *Analyze This* (1998), but Chase, his creative collaborators, and the stellar cast dig deep. As if commenting on those comedies, at one point Tony tells Dr. Melfi, *"I never really understood what* [it] *felt* [like], *to be used for somebody else's amusement like a f—g dancing bear"* (in episode ten, *"A Hit is a Hit"*). The Sopranos uses this narrative conceit to structure its dangerous power shifts and tragedies, to explore Tony's growing relationship with Melfi and his subsequent adaptive ability to analyze, grasp, and change his own perceptions as necssary. The series even plunders the dark dream realm of key characters with potent effect (during his DVD interview, Chase cites the influence here of directors like Luis Bunuel and David Lynch). Furthermore, savvy to its cultural roots and context, Chase and company constantly reflect upon how their portrait of organized crime thrives on the very pop icons that caricature it, and the toll of the 'information highway' on an environment so dependent on absolute secrecy and covert control (Tony's kids check the internet to verify Dad's mob connections).

Unlike so many other films and failed TV series, *The Sopranos* really *is* as good as its precursors, Mario Puzo's novel *The Godfather* and Francis Ford Coppola's film adaptations, Martin Scorsese's *Mean Streets* (1973) and *Goodfellas* (1990). As Chase says during his DVD commentary, "Goodfellas *is the Koran,"* and he peppered his cast with alumni of both *Goodfellas* (Braco, Michael Imperioli as Tony's nephew and heir-apparent Christopher, Tony Sirico as Paulie) and *Godfather II* (Sirico; Dominic Chianese as Uncle Junior) — not out of homage or hubris, but because all these performers were so right for their roles. What positions *The Sopranos* alongside those classic films, though, is its use of the expansive canvas of the TV series format to dissect, rather than trivialize, the real meat of its genre and respective story. It's the *I, Claudius* of its genre.

Maintaining a rigorous focus throughout its episodic presentation, the series chronicles the volatile reality of Tony's existence and the complex weave of sensibilities and lives around him (and particularly those dependent upon him) with a resonant depth few feature films ever approach. *The Sopranos* dissects the dynamic of both the family and 'The Family' with a sophisticated and riveting intimacy. Telling moments between husband and wife Carmela (Edie Falco), father and son Tony Jr. (Robert Iler), and father and daughter Meadow (Jamie-Lynn Sigler), are far more affecting, moving, and disturbing then those we've encountered before because we spend more time with, and know more about, these characters. Chase and his creative collaborators do not squander that investment (as most TV series do). We are shaken by Carmela's confession of her awful suspicions about, and knowing complicity with, her husband's true nature; Tony Jr.'s long, sober look at his father at a funeral as the truth of his family's connection to the mob sinks in; Meadow's attempt to have a heart-to-heart with Tony during their road trip to check out colleges, compromised by her father's inability to reveal his true nature (including the murder he has committed that very afternoon); the corrosive dynamic between Tony and his mother Livia, culminating in the attempt on his life and the final episode's confrontation between mother and son en route to the operating room. This is potent drama, in any medium. Highly Recommended!

Visually, the VHS and DVD sets are identical, though the latter is anamorphically enhanced. The DVD boxed set also adds some material that true Sopranophiles won't want to miss: an audio commentary on the pilot episode by series creator David Chase and actor/director Peter Bogdanovich (who now plays Dr. Melfi's own psychiatrist on the show), a 77m interview with Chase conducted by Bogdanovich on the set of Tony Soprano's kitchen, two promotional featurettes, and an episode log complete with previews and recaps. *(Unrated, but treat this as "R"-rated fare, for sometimes graphic violence, nudity and sexual situations, strong language, and truly adult content.)* [21]

Your reaction to ***SHAFT*** (2000), a lively remake of Gordon Parks' 1971 adaptation of Ernest Tidyman's tidy thriller, is entirely dependent on the baggage you do — or don't — bring to it. The original *Shaft* was a breakthrough mainstream film, a studio-financed (MGM) street-wise thriller about a black private detective (played by Richard Roundtree) helmed by a black director (who was also a premiere photographer, author, and gentleman) — a rarity in its time. The almost unprecedented spectacle of a contemporary urban black hero (anticipated by the unexpected success of Melvin Van Peebles' 1971 indy *Sweet Sweetback's Baadasssss Song* earlier that year, establishing the black outlaw as cultural anti-hero) strutting bigger-then-life on the silver screen galvanized a generation. *Shaft* opened the doors to fresh opportunities for black filmmakers and actors, as well as ruthless exploitation of the genre (i.e., *"blaxploitation"*) by lesser talents. *Shaft* spawned two lackluster sequels (*Shaft's Big Score*, 1972, and *Shaft in Africa*, 1973), but nothing could undermine the stature of the original.

---

[21] This review was also published in *The Video Watchdog* #71, May 2001, pp. 25-27.

Why make a new *Shaft*? I've often bemoaned the paucity of imagination and reverence brought to the plethora of Hollywood remakes we've endured of late (see last week's review of *Gone in 60 Seconds*, for instance). The new *Shaft* is a prime of example of a remake devoted to its source material, enthused to engage with such beloved roots, and eager to live up to its promise. Whatever the catalytic motivating factor here (the usual Hollywood need to fleece pre-sold expectations, no doubt), director John Singleton (*Boyz in the Hood*, 1991, *Higher Learning*, 1995, *Rosewood*, 1997, etc.) and star Samuel L. Jackson rise to the occasion with style, and *do* fill the mighty-big shoes of black brothers Parks and Roundtree quite nicely, thank you. They acknowledge and honor their debt to both, casting Roundtree as the real John Shaft, uncle to the remakes virile new model, and showcasing the elder Parks in a cameo in Harlem's famous Lenox Lounge (*"Mr. P, how you be?"*). This new *Shaft* embraces the mean streets of New York City, the leather jacket, the Isaac Hayes theme, and attitude to spare with its own feverish electricity, knowing that most of the fun here is seeing Samuel L. relish his in-your-face dialogue and physical confrontations with such absolute abandon. The man is getting to play one of his childhood heroes — you can see he loves every minute of it — and his passion is contagious, however derivative the vehicle.

The film opens with a jarring race-murder scene: the victim Trey (Mekhi Phifer) is a young, upscale urban black student who made the mistake of talking back to an affluent yuppie sociopath Walter Wade Jr. (Christian Bale, still in *American Psycho* mode), and had his skull staved in for his insolence. Shaft bristles at the loss, the killer's cold bravado, and the injustice of the favors extended to Wade Jr., who promptly skips bail and disappears for two years. Shaft is waiting for him when he returns. Managing to detain Wade Jr. in overnight lockup before the courts set him free again, Shaft inadvertently forges the unlikely bond between smug racist Wade Jr. and Dominican drug-gangster People Hernandez (Jeffrey Wright, chewing the scenery like Al Pacino in *Scarface*); united in their hatred for Shaft, the sparks fan into a fiery vendetta that soon spills into the streets. Caught in the crossfire is innocent Diane Palmieri (Toni Collette), reluctant witness to Trey's murder.

The original John Shaft was a private detective; Jackson's turn as that Shaft's nephew charts his career move from NYC cop to renegade jettisoning his badge to seek an unimpeded righting-of-monstrous-wrongs. Thus, *Shaft* is essentially another vigilante-justice scenario and just another black *Dirty Harry* after thirty years of similar variations on the theme. But he also bridges the cop-as-hero and gangsta-as-antihero archetypes polarized in the 1970s by the first *Shaft* and *Sweet Sweetback*; like I said, Singleton and Jackson know and honor their forefathers. The film's volatile mix of confrontational racism (in a scenario that accommodates contemporary stereotypes, like Shaft's comical Rastafarian sidekick played by Busta Rhymes), drug mayhem, bloody violence, and ultimate siding with vigilantism in the face of an utterly corrupt white judicial system is a deliberately abrasive concoction, and hardly suitable for all tastes. If you didn't see the original when it came out, or care a whit about its legacy, this new *Shaft* will most likely play as just another pumped-up cop movie offering a role model of dubious merit, but those who were there and/or do care with find much to savor here. And Samuel L. Jackson fans? Ah, you'll be in heaven for 99 minutes. *(Rated "R" for mucho violence, harsh language, alcohol and drug use and abuse, nudity, sexual situations, and its pro-vigilante stance.)*

December 21:

Canadian filmmaker Guy Maddin is among North America's most unique, idiosyncratic directors. Fascinated with the look, sound, pace, and textures of the twilight realm of the early sound era — the part-silent, part-sound efforts of the very late 1920s — Maddin roots his narratives and cinematic style in a deliberately archaic, anachronistic universe unlike any other. Kino Video has just re-released Maddin's bizarre debut feature ***TALES FROM THE GIMLI HOSPITAL*** (1986) and debuted ***CAREFUL*** (1997), offering adventurous viewers something truly different amid the endless slush pile of Hollywood tripe and trifles.

The stories, such as they are, are steeped in an odd, wholly-invented North country exoticism. *Gimli Hospital* is set in a neo-Scandanavian village in Manitoba, *"a Gimli we no longer know."* It's a frigid never-never land where the titular hospital is run by ghoulish surgeons and nurses, and cattle shivering in stalls beneath the floorboards provide what little warmth the beds provide. There, pestilence victims Einar the lonely (Kyle McCulloch) and Gunnar (Michael Gottli) become friends until the convoluted tangle of desire, reveries, and longing culminates in rivalry and a bloody duel.

Careful is nestled in the faux-European Alpine village of Tolzbad, where the tiniest sound could literally bring the snow-covered mountains down around the ears of the citizens. Life beneath the avalanche nurtures a fearful culture where sibling bonds are frayed by incestuous dreams, ghost visitations, and growing lunacy, prompting feuding brothers to grow increasingly reckless and court inevitable disaster.

Unrequited love, jealousy, murder, suicide, and revenge fuel these absurdist melodramas, punctuated by sometimes hilarious, occasionally horrific eruptions amid their highly-stylized emotional landscapes. These flourishes are lovingly muffled beneath layer upon layer of erratic sound, arch dialogue, exaggerated performances, grainy celluloid grit and grime, and (in *Careful*, Maddin's first color film) carefully-orchestrated color patinas and tints evocative of old illustrations or postcards of long-forgotten people and places. Maddin claims he has as many names for film textures as Eskimos do for snow, and this palette lends his films a uncanny flavor. They malinger in a moody, self-absorbed limbo evocative of barely-remembered fever dreams, unreeling like impressions of films unmade rather than actual films, or the kind of pre-VCR, pre-cable late-night television viewing that would wax and wane into static dependent on the weather or orientation of a rooftop antennae.

Maddin's sly dark humor is the icing on the cake. In *Gimli Hospital*, bark-cutting is the preferred folk art; grooming involves fish oil freshly-squeezed directly onto the hair; the only available anesthetic in the hospital are the morbid puppet shows performed by the hollow-eyed nurses. *Careful* revels in homespun homilies like *"Never gamble with life"* and *"Never hold a baby's face near an open pin!"* and demonstrates their virtue in Tolzbad's Freudian ice chest.

Gimli Hospital and *Careful* are strange, funny, moving, and quite beautiful works, though certainly *not* for all tastes. They will bore some viewers while absolutely mesmerizing others, and there's no telling which camp you'll fall into until you take the plunge (I love Maddin's films, but precious few of my friends share my affection for his work). Should you fall under his spell as I have, the Kino DVDs are particularly recommended, boasting rich transfers with nifty extras including Maddin's commentaries — accompanied on *Careful* by co-author George Toles — short films (including Maddin's first film *The Dead Father*, 1986), and a featurette on the making of his most recent feature, *Twilight of the Ice Nymphs* (1998), a marvelous (and as-yet unreleased) fable starring Alice Krige, Shelley Duvall, and Frank Gorshin. My Christmas wish is that Maddin's other films will soon be available on video, too. *(Both films are unrated, but are not for younger viewers, featuring sexual and adult situations, nudity, violence, and gore.)*

Maddin unapologetically plunges viewers into his arcane fantasies; those who prefer more traditional Hollywood submersion techniques will undoubtably gravitate to **THE CELL** (2000). Where Maddin's films are organically dreamlike in every way, *The Cell* is a glossy, gory, garish CGI-cartoon stitched to a familiar serial-killer potboiler which serves as a vehicle for music video director Tarsem Singh's visual imagination. Singh lavishes all manner of opulent, cutting-edge computer-generated imagery on an otherwise repellent scenario that recalls the sordid *Oxygen* (1999),[22] and employs the already old-hat trope of a woman's psychic link with the sexual predator (ala *Mind Over Murder*, 1979, *The Eyes of Laura Mars*, 1978, and — most recently — Neil Jordan's *In Dreams*, 1999).

---

[22] See *Blur, Vol. 1*, pp. 175-176.

A woman is kidnapped and imprisoned by necrophile Carl Stargher (Vincent D'Onofrio of *Full Metal Jacket*, 1987, *The Whole Wide World*, 1996, *Men in Black*, 1997, *Steal This Movie*, 2000, etc.). She has 40 hours to live before the ingenious glass-walled 'cell' fills with water and drowns her. The expected police procedural is derailed, however, when Stargher plunges into a coma moments before the FBI captures him, prompting the unlikely intervention of dream-therapist Catherine Deane (Jennifer Lopez of *Out of Sight*, 1998, *U-Turn* and *Selena*, both 1997, etc.) who must enter Stargher's terrifying dream reality in hopes of extracting the whereabouts of his latest victim. After 40 minutes of set-up, she does so, and the film nimbly crosscuts between the dire situation of Stargher's victim entombed in the literal cell and the increasingly grandiose and gruesome labyrinth of Stargher's internalized 'cell' of the mind. With the clock ticking, FBI agent Peter Novak (Vince Vaughn of *Swingers*, 1996, *Return to Paradise* and *Clay Pigeons*, both 1998, etc.) is forced to enter the nightmare realm, too, in order to rescue Catherine from their shared interior worlds.

Unlike other alumni of TV commercials and music videos, Singh is a supple storyteller. *The Cell* is a heady 'trip,' with top-notch technical credits, solid performances, and abundant eye-candy, including the ravishing 'Specialty Costumes' by Eiko Ishioka (who cops the 'sleep suits' from her own armor designs for Francis Ford Coppola's baroque 1992 version of *Bram Stoker's Dracula*). Melding the fantasy premises of 1980s gems like *Dreamscape* and *A Nightmare on Elm Street* (both 1984) and the escalating ghastliness of 1990s horrors like *Silence of the Lambs* (1991), *Se7en* (1995), and Fox TV's *Millennium* series (1996-99), *The Cell* aims to outstrip its precursors with its vivid extremes of emotional torture, physical (and self-inflicted) atrocities, and ornate evocations of nightmare netherworlds.

The mercurial visuals are often intoxicating, but only those with a taste for mayhem are likely to savor director Singh's dazzling bag of tricks (incorporating imagery from diverse sources like animators the Brothers Quay all the way to sculptor Mark Prent). Jean Cocteau, Luis Bunuel, David Lynch and Guy Maddin worked far greater wonders with none of the high-tech tools at the filmmakers' disposal here; exploitation (Stargher's victims remain mere ciphers, little more than the dolls he makes of them), not art, greases the wheels in this film, but it's a dazzling ride nonetheless.

The DVD is highly recommended, chock-full of extras and intensive behind-the-scenes production details viewable from multiple angles. *The Cell* was photographed in Super 35, so while New Line's 'Platinum Series' DVD release is appropriately letterboxed at 2.35:1 and anamorphically enhanced, the VHS release actually exposes more of the frame. Despite this, the fullscreen framing is not ideal; the shots of the protagonists suspended in their muscle suits, for instance, shows the nearest figure with their head and feet partially cropped. At the same time, by widening the aperture, this version can sometimes be more thrilling to the eye. The Dolby Surround mix (in 5:1 on the DVD) is superb, accentuating Howard Shore's inspired, Moroccan-flavored score. In addition to its rental-priced VHS release, *The Cell* is also the latest film to be released in New Line Home Video's always-extraordinary 'Platinum Series' of DVDs. Included are a commentary by director Singh, examinations of the special effects, art direction, makeup and costumes, various deleted scenes, and a *"brain map and empathy test."*

The Cell is a lively concoction, but it's *not* for squeamish or impressionable young viewers. *(Rated a strong "R" for graphic violence, gore, sadism, masochism and self-mutilation, harrowing glimpses of domestic and child abuse, strong language, nudity, deviant sexuality, and adult situations.)* [23]

ROAD TRIP is an amusing sophomoric (as in college) comedy from Todd Phillips, the auteur of (ahem) *Frat House* (1998), co-scripted by screen 'virgin' Scot Armstrong. Bad-boy cable star Tom Green relates and inhabits the tall tale of lovers-since-childhood Josh (Brekin Meyer) and Tiffany (Rachel Blanchard), whose ongoing long-distance relationship (he's in Texas, she's in Ithaca, NY) is in trouble. Josh has succumbed to temptation and the mistaken mailing of an incriminating video to Tiffany in place of Josh's intended 'love letter' cassette sets the minimal plot in motion. With only three days to race across country and intercept the tape, and the dubious moral support of his cronies (Seann William Scott, Paulo Costanzo, and DJ Qualls), Josh mounts a desperate road trip fueled by the usual nonsense: parents in pursuit, accidents, fraud, drugs, drink, sex, and the like.

Road Trip's characters are likable enough idiots, sexist stereotypes are championed and discarded as deemed necessary with opportunistic abandon, scatological humor is a staple (including the joys of proctological examination), and the usual 'rites of passage'

---

[23] This review was also published in *The Video Watchdog* #70, April 2001, pp. 13-15.

are chronicled with glee. Hard to believe that the truly subversive, anarchic *Animal House* (1978) has spawned such an endless torrent of vapid imitators, most of which (spearheaded by *Porky's*, 1982) mindlessly embraced the same teen-comedy stereotypes Animal House so energetically deflated.

Alas, *Road Trip* is just more of the same, though the high spirits the cast bring to it are contagious if you're young enough or in a party frame of mind. It's much more fun than either *Loser* or *Boys and Girls* (both 2000), recent releases which were truly appalling 'date movies' for braindead teens. Be warned, though, that *Road Trip* features a key story bit involving a classroom bomb scare (depicted here as an act of providence); it's a particularly irresponsible twist given the ongoing recent trouble with bomb threats at our area schools. Kids, don't try this at home. *(Rated "R" for language, casual alcohol and drug use, nudity, sexual situations, and some violence.)*

December 28:

"How did you give a medal to someone who doesn't exist for something that didn't happen?" muses United Nations Secretary General Douglas Thomas (Donald Sutherland) early on in Christian Duguay's **THE ART OF WAR** (2000), an artless but efficient thriller. Sutherland's effete politician is referring to the film's hero Shaw (Wesley Snipes), veteran agent for a "covert, unorthodox" peace-keeping unit acting on behalf of various UN interests. Snipes delivers his usual solid, no-nonsense presence and polish, but the film doesn't add up to much in the end.

The lively prologue finds Shaw coercing negotiations between North and South Korea at a gala gathering (using time-honored techniques of hidden surveillance devices, extortion, gunplay, gadgetry, and the little public martial arts exhibition). Thereafter, Shaw, his partner Bly (Michael Biehn), and boss Eleanor Hooks (Anne Archer) are plunged into the 'real dirt' behind the recent Chinese free-trade agreement... according to Hollywood, that is. A boxcar of dead Chinese refugees and the assassination of Chinese Ambassador Wu (played by familiar character actor James Hong) threaten to derail the pending agreement. In quick order, Shaw is framed for the killing; witness and UN interpreter Julia (Marie Matiko) becomes a target of the mysterious Asian triad apparently behind the butchery; and bedraggled FBI agent Frank Cappella (Maury Chaykin) is in hot pursuit of both. The film's nominal villain — among many, in the end — is triad kingpin David Chau (Cary-Hiroyuki Tagawa, a shoe-in after similar nastiness in *Mortal Kombat*, 1995, *The Phantom*, 1996, etc.), as the escalating body count, improbable stunts, and privileged internet access puts Shaw and Julia through their paces.

Canadian director Duguay kicked off his career with two passable sequels to David Cronenberg's *Scanners* almost a decade ago (later making one of the more inventive Philip K. Dick adaptations, *Screamers*, 1995). *The Art of War* is driven by similarly creaky *Scanners*-like plot mechanics: espionage, subterfuge, and conspiracies feed betrayal upon counter-betrayal, climaxing in increasingly violent setpieces. Observant viewers will find the casting alone a dead giveaway of the culpable parties, marking *The Art of War* as just another 1990s actioner that squanders its implied international arena as mere backdrop for just another high-testosterone shoot 'em up. *(Rated "R" for violence, gore, gunplay, nudity, language, adult and sexual content.)*

THE TERRORIST (***Theeviravaathi: The Terrorist***, 1999) is a film that lives up to the promise of the title *The Art of War*, detailing the reality of ongoing warfare and its terrible toll on those trapped in its cruel talons. India filmmaker Santosh Sivan (*Halo*, 1997, *Darmiyan*, 1997, *Dil Se.../From the Heart*, 1998, etc.) wrote, directed, and photographed *The Terrorist* with visionary passion and ruthless precision, detailing a few days — perhaps the final days — in the life of a nineteen-year-old young woman named Malli (Ayesha Dharkar).

The film opens with Malli's dispassionate execution of a traitor among her group of Indian freedom fighters; a devoted guerrilla warrior fighting in the revered shadow of her deceased father and brother's sacrifices for 'the cause,' Malli is clearly idolized by her fellow rebels. *"Valiant death"* and martyrdom is in her blood, it seems, and Santosh Sivan's camera lingers on her face and unflinching gaze. Her eyes are by turn curious and cold, reflecting the openness of her youth as well as the reptilian opacity of her sharpened killing instincts. When her superiors require a volunteer for a suicide bombing of a targeted official, Malli is eager to give her life to complete an *"assassination to shake the world."* Accepting the fatal assignation, Malli is told she is *"supreme... a thinking bomb."* But as the film unfolds, her strength becomes her dilemma.

Her passage from the turmoil of the guerrilla life — all she has ever known — to her late awakening in the final act is chronicled with mesmerizing immediacy. The first leg of Malli's journey puts her in the hands of a mere child named Lotus (a moving performance by

Vishwas), a mournful boy tormented by the loss of his family and the horrific violence around him. Ferrying to the target city, Malli is sheltered by an apparently vain, talkative farmer nicknamed 'Mad Vasu' (charmingly played by Parmeshwaran), lingering for four days under the guise of a traveling student. Given the room of Vasu's absent photojournalist son, the gallery of photos that adorn the walls offer a window on a world Malli has never dreamed existed, much less seen, while Vasu's generous spirit and hospitality provide her first taste of domestic comfort and harmony. Away from the constant warfare that constitutes her sum experience, the hitherto unconsidered potential of life itself begins to seduce Malli, prompting her to question her path — and thereby hangs the tale, with a couple of surprises along the way I will not betray here.

Malli's sojourn from bloodshed and irrevocable loss to a growing reverence and desire for life compromises her ongoing courtship with death. As Malli's decisive rendezvous with her target approaches, Sivan tells her story with poetic clarity and an eye and ear ever-attuned to its beauties. Never down-playing the tragic scope of Malli's passage, Sivan pauses throughout to capture the allure of a leaf sinking in a pool; rain water spinning on vegetation; blood soaking into gauze; a cloth mask spreading like a ghost in a river's current; Malli's hair twined around the finger of a love-struck wounded rebel (K. Krishna); beads of moisture on skin. *The Terrorist* is a ravishing, extraordinary motion picture, fueled by Ayesha Dharkar's marvelous central performance as Malli. This is without a doubt one of the year's best; highly recommended. *(Unrated, though its frank depiction of warfare, violence, death, adult and sexual content would most likely earn an "R" rating.)*

Okay, *PARTY!!* Here's a quick run-down of the New Year season's party entertainments:

GROOVE (2000) and ***HUMAN TRAFFIC*** (1999) both cover the 'rave' scene through the eyes of their youthful filmmakers, pumped by throbbing scores, energetic casts, and their respective cultural soups, and as such are of particular interest (if only as artifacts of this party-obsessed generation). Writer/director/editor Greg Harrison's *Groove* details the recipe and risk in mounting a rave from scratch, set in an abandoned San Francisco warehouse transformed under the steady hand of selfless organizer Ernie (Steve Van Wormer). Groove chronicles the highs and lows of its single evening's events with a knowing embrace of the positive transformative potential and listless self-destructive edge of its nomadic nightclub community. Harrison's fidelity and attention to his characters is engaging, offering viewers who live outside such circles (like myself) entry to its select wonders through neophyte David (Hamish Linklater), a reluctant and inexperienced party-goer dragged along by his brother Colin (Denny Kirkwood) and Colin's girlfriend Harmony (Mackenzie Firgens). Left to his own devices amid the procession of DJs, vinyl, 'A', 'E', and bottled water, David gravitates to Leyla (Lola Claudine), who becomes his guide and — before the evening is over — much more. *Groove* offers an affectionate snapshot and celebration of its scene, and as such is well worth a look.

Across the Atlantic, Justin Kerrigan's *Human Traffic* charts the *British* rave scene via its clutch of partygoers. Our designated narrator is Jip (John Simm), a slim lad plagued with a job he loathes, a hooker mom, and a case of 'Mr. Floppy' compromising his sex life. With his eye on man-wary Lulu (Lorraine Pilkington), Jip's weekend out in Cardiff with Lulu, jealous best buddy Koop (Shaun Parkes), Koop's girlfriend Nina (Nicola Reynolds), her little brother Lee (Dean Davies), and the perpetually drug-addled Moff (Danny Dyer) is the sum and substance of the film. Your level of engagement with this rag-tag crew will determine your like or dislike of the film itself, which wants to mount the intense identification *Trainspotting* (1996) earned in spades by pirating that much-better-film's devices. Thus, Jip is constantly talking to the camera; cinematographer David Bennett relies a bit much on distorting lenses to evoke the ecstacy-enhanced perspective of events; comedic spots interrupt the narrative with channel-surfing non-sequiters like Moff's chat with *"Reality"* and a detour on *"spliff politics"*; *lots* of pop-cultural patter (including an interminable rant about *Star Wars*) pepper the proceedings. In the wind down, *Human Traffic* ends up being as old-fashioned and soft-hearted about romance as *Groove*, demonstrating however much the trappings may change, the song remains the same. Of the two, I preferred *Groove*, but give 'em both a game go.

SAVING GRACE (2000) is a party movie for old-timers, dabbling with marijuana and its giddy effects as a substitute for the alcoholic spirits that fired the antics in venerable UK comedies of yore. Despite its Cheech and Chong situational comedy, *Saving Grace* aspires to the heights of *Tight Little Island* (aka *Whiskey Galore*, 1949, a truly great comedy that remains, alas, long out-of-print on video) and more immediate contemporaries like *Waking Ned Devine* (1999),[24] but it falls short.

When widow Grace Trevethyn (Brenda Blethyn) is left unexpectedly destitute by her husband's passing (the conniving blighter leaves her only ever-mounting debts), her well-intentioned Scotsman gardener Matthew (Craig Ferguson) turns Grace's green thumb to a high-yield crop of contraband hemp. True to its genre, Grace's non-malicious flirtation with criminality is quietly applauded and supported by the citizenry. *"Kind of warms the heart,"* wall-eyed bartender Charlie (Paul Brooke) wistfully sighs, *"Grace carrying on the local tradition of complete and utter contempt for the law."* Local color delivered by the solid cast and setting (filmed in Cornwall and Port Isaac) lends cozy charm to the increasingly predictable and silly proceedings as Brenda Blethyn's performance as Grace anchors the film (but scores only one truly moving moment in her first encounter with dead hubby's mistress Honey Chambers, played by Diana Quick).

Saving Grace is ultimately another lame drug caper by filmmakers who, apparently, never inhaled. The effects of marijuana are ridiculously exaggerated for easy laughs throughout, though the bout of munchies suffered by two elder shopkeepers (Phyluda Law and Linda Kerr Scott) sipping marijuana tea is amusing. To the film's detriment, the sly humor — the local vicar's nervous midnight viewing of a Hammer *Dracula* film, Grace's off-handed fly-casting advice to crimelord Jacques Chavalier (Tcheky Karyo) — is buried by the *Reefer Madness* nonsense, but undemanding viewers will have a painless dose of fun nevertheless. *(Rated "PG-13" for*

---

[24] See *Blur, Vol. 1*, pg. 29.

language, abundant drug use and references, and some adult and sexual content.)

I covered *Road Trip* last week, which remains the party-movie of choice for teenagers this weekend. ***SCARY MOVIE*** (2000) is its only real contender. Like all such parodies in the scatter shot *Airplane!* and *Naked Gun* mode — with their roots firmly embedded in Harvey Kurtzman's 1950s *Mad* comics and the later *Mad* magazine's movie satires — *Scary Movie* either works for you or it doesn't, and its effects are considerably enhanced by an appropriately noisy, festive, receptive audience to share the laughs.

Appropriating the originally announced title for Wes Craven's surprise shocker *Scream* (1996), *Scary Movie* puts the thumbscrews to the entire *Scream* franchise and its opportunistic offspring (*Urban Legends, I Know What You Did Last Summer*, etc.) and precursors. Along the way, the Wayans Brothers (co-writers Shawn and Marlon, who also play lead roles, and director Keenan Ivory) also lampoon *Basic Instinct, The Matrix, The Blair Witch Project, The Sixth Sense*, and — in one jaw-droppingly explicit and hilarious sex scene — both the fountain of gore that marked Johnny Depp's bedtime demise in the original *A Nightmare on Elm Street* (1984) and the patented 'money shot' of all XXX fare.[25] As

---

[25] I'll spell out here what I couldn't in a family newspaper, as this is still the single most outrageous sex shot I've ever seen in an 'R' rated movie: instead of the geyser of blood that erupted from Depp's bed in *A Nightmare on Elm Street*, *Scary Movie*'s bed scene pins its hapless teen against the ceiling in a graphic 'Old Faithful' of semen! Nothing in any subsequent horror movie satire even comes (pun intended) close.

Keenan Ivory Wayans notes in the DVD extras, *Scary Movie* is *"a spoof of a satire"* (as *Scream* did, after all, level its own brand of satire at the genre), a tightwire-walk that prompts the Wayans to pull out all the stops in their scatological savaging of the *"teen scream"* scene.

I don't want to cramp anybody's party plans, but parents should be warned that this is the most explicitly sexual 'R'-rated comedy in Hollywood history, with more bodily fluids on screen than the MPAA has ever indulged before. En route, the Wayans offer some truly startling sight gags, including the character of gym coach Miss Mann (played by Jayne Trcka, who also appeared as the androgynous being in the first killer dream sequence in *The Cell*), a gross nod to the genre's venerable pantheon of gender-confused caricatures (from *Psycho*, 1960, and *Homicidal*, 1961, through Russ Meyer's *Beyond the Valley of the Dolls*, 1970, and 1981 slashers like *Terror Train* and *Sleepaway Camp*). But, hey, it *is* the year 2000 — and we all knew we were on this road once audiences cheered *There's Something About Mary*'s raucous laughs. The DVD boasts an additional six cut scenes as *"The Goods"* on its menu; most of the trims feature minor but salacious gags. *Scary Movie* is rude, crude, and lewd — but damn, it's funny, and hands-down the best party movie of the New Year. *(Rated a very strong "R" for more things than I can mention in a family newspaper.)*

December 28: A Good Year's Crop: Top-20 Videos of 2000

1999 and 2000 were a remarkable year for movies in general, and American films in particular. That was borne out in this year's prime bumper crop of video releases, which capped the 20th Century — the first one hundred years of American film-making — with style to spare. So, the 20th Century's passing, commemorated with twenty films from the past year.

Here's my personal (very personal) picks of the litter. All of us, no doubt, have our own particular favorites, and I'm sorry if I passed up a favorite of yours. As they say, one man's meat is another one's poison, meaning I've no doubt listed one or two titles you might put on your own *"Worst of 2000"* list. Still, it was difficult to keep it down to only twenty — from non-movies I had to disqualify (the first season of HBO's classic series *The Sopranos*) to unpretentious delights like the inspired *The 13th Warrior* and *Galaxy Quest*, an exhilerating sf comedy that was almost shelved by its parent studio — there were so many other I wish I could have included. It really was a tremendous year, full of surprises; don't let anyone tell you otherwise. My top-20 list (in alphabetical, not preferential, order) also lists the dates of each respective entry's full review in the *Reformer* that I'm quoting from, for those of you who care to ferret out the complete reviews. Happy New Year, one and all; may 2001 be an even better year for you and yours... and, of course, video viewing!

(1) *ALL ABOUT MY MOTHER*: When her 17-year-old son is killed in an accident, Manuela (Cecilia Roth) abandons her professional life in Madrid and plunges into Barcelona's fringe element in search of Estaban's long-lost father (a seductive transsexual known as Lola). En route, Manuela connects with an entirely new reorientation to life. *"Pedro Almodovar's best work crackles with lively, engaging characters and situations, eye-drugging set and costume designs, and inventive* *narrative twists that reminds one how lifeless and unimaginative most American films truly are.* All About My Mother *certainly ranks among Almodovar's finest efforts... infusing this sensual melodrama and latest cast of playful polymorphs with a fresh sense of sincerity and tenderness. ...Mothers, daughters, lesbians, transsexuals, transvestites, prostitutes: Almodovar engages with them all with an insouciant wit, vigor, and affection that is irresistible...* [celebrating] *the grace, elan, and empathy with which his characters negotiate their way through the roughest emotional seas. As the final credits announce, this is Almodovar's valentine to motherhood and women (however biologically artificial) everywhere, and well worth sharing."* (July 27)[26]

(2) *AMERICAN BEAUTY*: Major new talents Alan Ball (script) and Sam Mendes (director) blew away audiences and swept the Academy Awards with this suburban angst epic, starring Kevin Spacey as an adrift middle-aged family man at the end of his rope, lashing out in all directions while nurturing unsavory sexual fantasies about his daughter's cheerleading classmate (Mena Suvari). "American Beauty *cuts to the core of our cultural malaise with surgical precision, dissecting the ties that bind, the desires that debase, the urges that can enlighten and destroy in the same blink of an eye. It is devastatingly funny, oddly moving, utterly mesmerizing, unshakably disturbing — and absolutely essential viewing. ...For all its irony and ire,* American Beauty's *heart beats fierce and true....This is a rare, remarkable film, highly recommended for mature and adult viewers."* However, one caveat: *"A heartfelt warning to sur-*

---

[26] See *Blur, Vol. 2*, pp. 146-148.

vivors of child abuse: ...the screen time dedicated to an adult male's fixation on an underage teenage girl, and film's amoral tone and subjective depiction of this volatile element, may be painful and/or highly objectionable to survivors. Please, approach this film with caution, or avoid it altogether." (May 11).[27]

(3) *AMERICAN PSYCHO:* Mary Harron's inspired adaptation of Bret Easton Ellis' reviled 1991 novel is the year's most savage black comedy in a year filled with them. It is also a brilliant movie, an essential companion piece to Harron's earlier *I Shot Andy Warhol* (1996). *"Among the film's canniest moments are the showdowns between its perfectly coiffed suit-and-tie Wall Street merger-and-acquisitions professionals, challenging each other with their business cards like gunfighters in a Sergio Leone spaghetti western.... Though Harron necessarily downplays the graphic extremes of Ellis' novel (which would have never been permitted to reach the screen if filmed verbatim from the text), the progression of Bateman's crimes is clear... Sans his rage and the murders, Bateman feels no distinction from those he is so openly contemptuous and covetous of. This is the black heart of the film, essential to unraveling its disorienting final act... Harron ruthlessly exposes the seething corruption of* American Psycho's *chameleon yuppies and the frail females in their orbit."* (two-part review, Sept. 7-14)[28]

---

[27] See *Blur, Vol. 2*, pp. 61-63.
[28] See *Blur, Vol. 2*, pp. 189-203, 230, and the expanded essay version in a forthcoming volume of *Gooseflesh*, from Black Coat Press.

(4) *BEING JOHN MALKOVICH*: The oddest Hollywood film of the year is also one of the best. Don't let the synopsis put you off: A sadsack puppeteer (John Cusack) finds a tiny door hidden behind a file cabinet and enters, finding himself plopped into the skull of actor John Malkovich (playing himself) for 15 minutes of vicarious fame before being dumped along the NJ turnpike. He tells a co-worker (Catherine Keener) and his dumpy wife (Cameron Diaz), who exploit the find in unexpected ways. *"Charlie Kaufman's delirious, perfectly-tuned screenplay is that rare item, a true original. Rarer still,* [director Spike] *Jonze... and the remarkable cast strike and sustain precisely the right chord somewhere betwixt Lewis Carroll, Preston Sturges, and David Lynch. I can honestly say you've never seen anything quite like it, nor will you soon shake its lingering aftertaste. It's a miracle this film was made at all, given the enormous odds...Miracles do happen, though, and* Being John Malkovich *offers an evening of giddy entertainment to those willing to take the plunge."* (May 4) [29]

(5) *BOYS DON'T CRY*: *"Kimberley Peirce's compelling, loving, and fierce feature directorial debut showcases actress Hilary Swank's rivetting Academy Award-winning performance as Teena Brandon aka 'Brandon Teena,' the Nebraskan trans-gender whose self-transformation from young woman into young man ended in tragedy... Peirce (and co-screenwriter Andy Bienen) brilliantly weave the true story's complex emotional tapestry into a coherent, profoundly moving threnody... an extraordinary testimonial to Brandon's quest for transformation and transcendence, true love*

---

[29] See *Blur, Vol. 2*, pp. 54-55.

and acceptance, and all its attendent pleasure and pain, succor and release. They capture the rush amid the risk, the joy amid the sorrow, and lend what could have been an unbearably downbeat experience considerable heart. ...There's never been a film quite like this before, and I urge you to see it." Also see the documentary *The Brandon Teena Story* (see review, Feb. 3),[30] which chronicles the real story. (April 20)[31]

(6) *THE FIGHT CLUB:* David Fincher's masterful adaptation of Chuck Palahniuk's debut novel *"certainly isn't for everyone — its excessive mayhem, relentless kinetics, sneaky subliminals, and subversive agenda will put off many viewers — but it was one of last year's best and most under-rated films. Fincher has evolved into one of the current generation's most uncompromising visionary filmmakers... [a] genuinely heady, transformative experience. ...Fight Club delivers one hell of a rollercoaster ride as its lead characters pursue their obsessions to a truly cataclysmic ground zero. ...It must be seen and experienced on its own terms — and unless you have an aversion to the often brutal, in-your-face violence and aggression* Fight Club *necessarily revels in, I highly recommend you take the plunge."* (April 27)[32]

(7) *GHOST DOG: THE WAY OF THE SAMURAI:* The sleeper of the year, and the most inspired riff on the crime genre in ages, brimming with marvelously vivid characterizations. *"The latest from fiercely-independent American director Jim Jarmusch is true to*

---

[30] See *Blur, Vol. 1*, pp. 195-196.
[31] See *Blur, Vol. 2*, pp. 43-45.
[32] See *Blur, Vol. 2*, pp. 49-50.

the deadbeat rhythms, cool, wit, and vigor of his best work... melding Eastern philosophy and archetypes, urban hip hop culture, dysfunctional gangster stereotypes, and classical Western setpieces with mesmerizing insouciance. ...Despite the thrust of the plot, this is hardly a cops-and-crooks action movie: it's sheer poetry." (August 24)[33]

(8) *THE INSIDER:* Some say that timely 'issue' driven movies never stand the test of time, but Michael Mann's latest masterpiece strikes me as much more than just a sharp spin on a current hot-button topics (the tobacco industry scandal, the demise of TV journalism). It's a brilliant contemporary film noir, and Russell Crowe's central 'everyman' performance as the whistle-blower at the heart of the storm elevates this into rarified cinematic turf. *"...this remarkable film offers an intensive dissection of how barely-checked corporate power in 'the information age' can and does implacably target and destroy lives to protect or further their own agenda. ...The Insider demonstrates just how such corruptive forces work...a vivid, vitally important story brilliantly told....It's sobering, to say the least, to vicariously experience* [the whistle-blower's] *agonies for knowing and speaking a fundamental truth (in the end, all the suffering was orchestrated to prevent the uttering of a single sentence). Precious few American filmmakers could bring such incisive intelligence and dramatic clarity to the realities of big business, closed-door power brokers, legal warfare, and the very real toll such events take upon their active participants and nominal victims. Thankfully, director Michael Mann... is up to the task...*

---

[33] See *Blur, Vol. 2*, pp. 177-178.

tell[ing] *the tale with uncanny lucidity and skill...The struggle pitting the most fundamental of individual human needs — health, sanity, dignity, safety, family, the ability to work and earn a living — against the voracious appetites and interests of the ever-growing multinational corporations is among the most frightening facing us in this new Millennium. By addressing this subject with such clarity and candor,* The Insider *stands tall."* (April 13)[34]

(9) *JESUS' SON:* In the plethora of weekly new releases demanding attention, it's easy to pass up a gold nugget amid the heavily-marketed studio titles, where dross like *28 Days* (the dreadful Sandra Bullock rehab soaper)[35] fills an entire display wall and a masterpiece like ***Jesus' Son*** is consigned to two copies buried on the new release wall. This excellent film never scored a proper review from this writer, an oversight I will now rectify. New Zealand director Alison Maclean (*Crush*, 1992) brings her all to this compassionate, unflinching portrait of a gentle mid-American heroin addict (Billy Crudup) adrift in the 1970s, his painful odyssey, and his slow spiritual awakening to the world and his place in it. The deceptively anecdotal, staccato rhythms of the film capture the mellow protagonist's hazy off-and-on engagement with reality (including apparent continuity errors that capture his memory lapses and the constant reinvention of his personal history), but the beauty of the film lies in its lucid recognition that Crudup's character is a good soul struggling through all the lowlife perils of the addict lifestyle (thievery, violence, detox agonies,

---

[34] See *Blur, Vol. 2*, pp. 34-37.
[35] See *Blur, Vol. 2*, pp. 208-210.

AA meetings, etc.). Its attentive devotion to his crawl toward redemption is unexpectedly profound, funny, touching, and rewarding, making this necessary viewing. The title comes from the Velvet Underground/Lou Reed song *'Heroin'* (*"...when I'm rushing on my run, I feel just like Jesus' Son..."*), and the film is adapted from the short stories of Denis Johnson (who has a jarring cameo as an emergency room patient with a knife in his eye, being ministered to by a manic Jack Black); this is a kindred spirit to Gus Van Sant's *Drugstore Cowboy* (1989) and *My Own Private Idaho* (1991). Amid the viciously punitive anti-drug rhetoric of contemporary society, it's too easy to forget that life overwhelms and confuses good people all the time, and we all make choices that haunt us forever. *Jesus' Son* is the most remarkable indy film of the year, and Billy Crudup's central performance is a revelation, with ample support from Samantha Morton (as Crudup's ill-fated girlfriend), Denis Leary, Holly Hunter, Will Patton, Greg Germann, the previously mentioned Jack Black (*"listen to my shoes!"*), and Dennis Hopper. Lots of highly quotable lines, too (*"All this work is messing with my high"*). *(Not reviewed before now)*[36]

(10) *JOE THE KING:* Another unsung, sobering, quietly heartbreaking masterpiece; like its teenage protagonist, the film was neglected by everyone, though it's not to be missed. *"The devastation of disintegrating marriages and broken homes is the core of actor Frank Whaley's impressive directorial debut... chronicling the steady slide toward juvenile hall endured by unwashed*

---

[36] See the footnote ending this column; this is in fact the first publication of the *Jesus' Son* review.

14-year-old Joe (Noah Fleiss), who ineffectually assumes the titular moniker in one of his feeble attempts to keep his footing and a shred of dignity in a decidedly unfriendly world. At the bottom of the pecking order in every corner of his existence...Joe survives by staying below the radar as best he can. He indulges in petty crime and theft to stay afloat as he suffers the verbal and physical assaults ....Joe's unyielding stoicism, his relationship with his older brother Mike (Max Ligoshi), and attempt to find some kind of redemption and a niche for himself remains the absolute focus of Whaley's screenplay and direction. Highly recommended!" Val Kilmer, John Leguizamo, and Ethan Hawke also star. (Feb. 17)[37]

(11) *MAGNOLIA:* The latest from director Paul Thomas Anderson (*Boogie Nights*, 1997) remains *"an incredible film that weaves a complex tapestry of dramatic vignettes and characterizations into an organic whole that is more than the sum of its parts... to track the complex connections between nine people (and their many associates and acquaintances) in a single, fateful 24-hour period in San Fernando Valley, California. A remarkable cast (including Tom Cruise, Jason Robards, Julianne Moore, John C. Reilly, Philip Seymour Hoffman, William H. Macy, and many more) bring these people to vivid life as they interact in unexpected ways, each stumbling toward their respective redemption, damnation, or oblivion. ...*Magnolia *is a demanding but rewarding masterpiece. It isn't everyone's cup of tea; its unflinching dissection of human foibles and frailties will have many of you squirming — as will the revelatory climax, which establishes* Magnolia *as one of the few*

---

[37] See *Blur, Vol. 1*, pg. 205.

*truly Fortean films ever made. ...*Magnolia *is a challenging, audacious, entertaining, ravishing experience, a key work...in a bracing new era of American cinema."* (August 10)[38]

(12) *MY MOTHER'S EARLY LOVERS:* Vermont filmmaker Nora Jacobson's film version of Sybil Smith's as-yet unpublished autobiographical memoir (c'mon, local publishers — what are you waiting for?) is *"a potent drama, eschewing nostalgia and romanticism to unravel its tangled, troubled generational tapestry with moving clarity and sometimes startling emotional impact....Belying its modest means,* My Mother's Early Lovers *boasts a rich luster, narrative density, and emotional intensity that puts Hollywood to shame."* (October 19) [39]

(13) *PRINCESS MONONOKE:* Don't miss this *"marvelous anime epic, a feature-length animated fantasy from Japan's premiere animator and fantasist Hayao Miyazaki."* It's an *"energetic, engaging, breathtaking creation... [depicts the] escalating violence between the forces of man and nature, and the mystical primal being which lives in the deepest regions of the forest. This dense, powerful saga is a genuine epic in every sense of the word, tapping potent mythic wellsprings to explore fundamental issues of man and nature, technology and ecology, darkness and light.... like*

---

[38] See *Blur, Vol. 2*, pp. 162-164.

[39] A revised and expanded revision of the October, 2000 review of *My Mother's Early Lovers* has already been reprinted in my book *Green Mountain Cinema I* (Black Coat Press, 2004), hence its exclusion from the *Blur* series.

all of Miyazaki's work, Princess Mononoke *constructs and probes its invented universe with the moral rigor and complexity live-action Japanese filmmakers like Akira Kurosawa bring to their best work. There are no easy dualistic definitions of good and evil: each side of the struggle has their own goals, beliefs, and hard-earned prejudices, and the morality play is punctuated by surprising shifts in allegiance as Miyazaki's characters struggle to understand and/or control the awesome forces at work.... This is a magnificent film."* (August 31)[40]

(14) *THE SIXTH SENSE:* Writer/director M. Night Shyamalan's third feature is *"...a return to the evocatively suggestive horror film aesthetic established by producer Val Lewton in the 1940s...* The Sixth Sense *is a horror movie — more specifically, a ghost story — but it plucks your nerves en route to the heart, arriving at a lovingly-orchestrated final act that is as profoundly moving as it is terrifying.... Shyamalan's tale is blessed with ideal casting, particularly that of eleven-year old Haley Joel Osment, who... conjures real screen magic here. The ingenious tale, performances, and every aspect of the production rewards repeat viewings."* (March 30)[41]

(15) *SNOW FALLING ON CEDARS:* A post-WW2 murder trial in a small seaside village in the Pacific Northwest embroils a young reporter (Ethan Hawke) in the fate of the Japanese-American woman (Youki Kudoh), both harboring their own secrets and

---

[40] See *Blur, Vol. 2*, pp. 181-187.
[41] See *Blur, Vol. 1*, pp. 250-252.

recovering from personal tragedies linked to the War. Along with *The Straight Story* (see #16, below), this was the most profound romance of the year. *"...director Scott Hicks (*Shine*) mounts an evocative adaptation of David Guterson's best-selling novel of first love, truth, racism, and tragedy set amid one of recent American history's most shameful chapters. ...Hicks orchestrates these elements with consummate skill and a ravishing cinematic eye and ear....*Snow Falling on Cedars *never misses a step, deftly drawing its threads together with grace and resonant clarity. ...In a culture obsessed with delineating love almost exclusively in sexualized or familial terms, it is unusual to find such an honest and uncluttered expression of the most fragile of virtues we hold dear."* (June 1)[42]

(16) *THE STRAIGHT STORY:* David Lynch and Disney Studios — who'da thunk it? Together, they made a gem, *"...a cinematic haiku: short, simple, from and to the heart....lovingly channeling the restless spirits of American filmmaking masters John Ford and Preston Sturges...In an era defined by ironic cynicism, Lynch's most perversely subversive attribute may be his resolute naivete and refusal to indulge in cynicism, easy distance from the heart and hurt of life. ...*The Straight Story *lives up to its title telling the true story of Alvin Straight (Richard Farnsworth), a frail old fellow who sojourns from Iowa to Wisconsin on a lawnmower in hopes of mending the fences with his brother, though they haven't spoken in years. On the way, Alvin touches many hearts and lives....The tale unfolds with an unpretentious stoicism that keeps Farnsworth's character in absolute fo-*

---

[42] See *Blur, Vol. 2*, pp. 85-88.

cus. His soulful eyes brim with an affection for life and people, shadowed by past scars, regrets, and the sure knowledge of his own impending death. They quietly burn with the need to make amends with those nearest and dearest to him before time runs out. ...Lynch's vision remains as clear and resolute as the old man's until the final, masterfully understated moment. ...This is Lynch's most beautiful and accessible work, and one of the most lovely American films ever made." (May 11)[43]

(17) *THE TERRORIST:* A sensuous, sinewy, poetic portrait of a 19-year old girl who dedicates her final days to a suicide-bombing mission, only to taste the potential of a life in reach — but beyond her experience — as the minutes tick closer, closer to her death. A quietly moving, visually ravishing masterpiece. (see this week's review!)

(18) *THREE KINGS:* Hard to believe director David O. Russell has already forged the best anti-war film of the decade out of the debris of the Gulf War, but he has. A quartet of U.S. soldiers go on a treasure hunt, risking an international scandal in hopes of grabbing $40 million of Saddam Hussein's buried gold, only to become the reluctant protectors of a band of refugees and prisoners en route to the Iranian border. *"A biting, bracing, absurdist epic... Though it's deceptively energetic, spry, and often wickedly funny, the film quickly transcends its* Kelly's Heroes-*like caper comedy premise to join the ranks of genuinely subversive war classics... nothing in* [Russell's] *earlier satiric work suggested the expansive physical and political scope, much less the*

---

[43] See *Blur, Vol. 2*, pp. 66-68.

*kinetic cinematic assurance and edge, of this masterpiece. ...*Three Kings *mounts a vivid and pointed attack on that shameful war ...Be warned that the violence, when it erupts, is explicit — as it* must *be — but never gratuitous or glamorized. Highest recommendation!"* (April 13)[44]

(19) *TOY STORY 2:* The toys were back, with the *Toy Story* computer-generated animated ensemble still led by the vocal performances of Tom Hanks and Tim Allen in a rare sequel that improved on a rare original. *"The Pixar artists are not only brilliant technicians and innovative pioneers, they are among the finest storytellers in America, period.... directors John Lasseter, Lee Unkrich, and Ash Brannon dance circles around most live-action filmmakers....*Toy Story 2 *juggles the playful and profound with high spirits and razor-sharp wit, timing, and characterizations.... This is a magnificent film by any standard, not to be missed."* (November 23)[45]

(20) *THE WAR ZONE:* Given the perverse lionization of *American Beauty*'s pedophile 'hero', this heartbreaking portrait of adult-child sexual predation and its horrific consequences couldn't be more timely, essential, or necessary. *"Tim Roth's quietly harrowing feature-film directorial debut* [is] *an unflinching dissection of the corrosive impact incest has on a London family who uproot and move to a remote seaside residence.... Roth cuts to the heart with the precision of a surgeon.... charts the echoes of abuse across genera-*

---

[44] See *Blur, Vol. 2*, pp. 37-40.
[45] See this volume, pp. 32-34.

tional lines.... we cannot look away as the fragile illusions the family sustains are shattered in the wake of the awful truth. The film concludes with one of the most chilling final shots in recent memory." (August 17)[46]

---

[46] See *Blur, Vol. 2*, pp. 169-170. Note: Due to space constraints on the New Year section, this column was published in slightly truncated form in *The Brattleboro Reformer* as *"Year 2000 brought forth a good crop of videos,"* listing only 15 of the 20 titles I'd chosen; A&E editor Willow Dannible permitted me to edit that lineup down, trimming *All About My Mother, Jesus' Son, Joe the King, The Terrorist*, and *The War Zone*. Damn, I hated to see my review of *Jesus' Son* go. Portions of the above column also appeared in *The Chicopee Herald*, January 10-16, 2001, pg. 23.

2001

January 4:

The New Year — and New Millennium — has arrived with a pair of old-fashioned ghouls in tow. First up is Warner Brothers' prestige release of ***THE EXORCIST: THE VERSION YOU'VE NEVER SEEN*** (1973, revised and expanded in 2000), arriving just as the temperature outside approximates the chill in the bedroom of the possessed child Regan MacNeil (Linda Blair). It's worth a revisit, and not just for the thirteen revisions director William Friedkin has added in hindsight.

A little background: In January 1949, a 13-year-old boy in Mt. Rainier, Maryland (apparently troubled by the death of a beloved aunt) exhibited increasingly bizarre, self-destructive behavior that eluded medical diagnosis or treatment. In desperation, his parents called upon their local Lutheran Reverend Miles Schulze in February, who confirmed the boy's symptoms (while noting apparent poltergeist and telekinetic activity) and subsequently referred the family to Father E. Albert Hughes of Mt. Rainier's St. James Roman Catholic Church. Under instructions of the regional Archbishop, Father Hughes performed the Catholic ritual of exorcism on the boy in Georgetown University Hospital. The ritual was terminated when Hughes was injured. In March, the family moved in with relatives in St. Louis, Missouri, where a Father Bishop of St. Louis University, Father William Bowdern of St. Francis Xavier Church, and theological student Walter H. Halloran eventually completed the exorcism in St. Louis' Alexian Brothers' Hospital in April. According to witnesses, after manifestations of scratches, writing, and images of the devil *"drawn"* into the boy's flesh (amid bouts of spitting, blasphemous language, and ongoing telekinetic displays) during the final exorcism, the boy spoke with a voice identifying itself as St. Michael the Archangel and uttered the word *"Dominus"* (Lord). A loud report like a gunshot was heard throughout the ward as the boy's possession ended.

Was the Mt. Rainier case one of genuine possession? The names, places, and dates are indeed documented. The more fantastic elements are not, though its legacy stubbornly remains. Reporter Bill Brinkley declared the incident *"perhaps one of the most remarkable experiences of its kind in recent religious history."*[47] The case was later detailed in Thomas B. Allen's book *Possessed: The True Story of an Exorcism* (1993) and dramatized in Charles Vanderpool's Discovery Channel documentary *In the Grip of Evil* (1997). However, journalist Mark Opsasnick investigated the account, tracking down and speaking to the now-adult boy and his friends and family. Writing up his investigation for *Strange Magazine* (#20, 1998) and *The Fortean Times* (#123, July 1999), Opsasnick concluded that the boy had indeed suffered a prolonged emotional event that was medically untreated and dealt with via exorcism by church officials, but *"there is not one shred of hard evidence to support the notion of demonic possession."*[48]

Author William Peter Blatty was an undergraduate at Georgetown University when the Mt. Rainier case was reported in the newspapers. Blatty subsequently re-

---

[47] *"Ritual of Exorcism Repeated: Priest Frees Mt. Rainier Boy Reported Held in Devil's Grip," The Washington Post*, Saturday, August 20, 1949, page 1.
[48] Opsasnick, *The Fortean Times* #123, July 1999.

searched this case and wrote the novel *The Exorcist* (1971), crafting a fictionalized account by changing the gender of the child and embellishing its horrors while exploring the core issues of philosophy and religious belief which fascinated the former theological student. The novel immediately scored on the bestseller list and the screen rights were snapped up by Warner Bros. Given Blatty's prior experience as a screenwriter,[49] the studio agreed that Blatty himself script and produce the film, working with director William Friedkin. With important creative contributions by makeup master Dick Smith and veteran actress Mercedes McCambridge (providing the voice of the demon), the filmmakers crafted a vision of demonic possession that captivated and terrified audiences around the world.

The film version of *The Exorcist* had its world premiere in multiple theaters across the country on December 26th, 1973 (hence its re-release of the current revised video the same day in 2000), playing to capacity audiences. The transformation of young Regan (Linda Blair) into a hideously scarred, golden-eyed demon-child — indulging in blasphemous language and behavior, projectile vomiting, bone-crunching 360-degree head-spinning, and more — was unlike anything ever seen before. The horrors were tactile, almost palpable, and rendered with utter conviction. Friedkin also employed a nerve-jangling audio mix and occasional 'subliminal' images (including single frames of a demonic face provided by Blair's stunt double Eileen Dietz, that aficionados dubbed 'Captain Howdy') to orchestrate a startlingly

---

[49] Blatty had previously scripted or scored writing credits on eight features, including *A Shot in the Dark* (1964) and *Gunn* (1967).

fresh modern horror epic. There were reports of audience members vomiting, fleeing, or fainting, which only attracted larger crowds, as did the lurid press and studio publicity concerning mysterious events that had plagued the supposedly 'cursed' production.

The curse apparently did not extend to its earnings, as it broke international boxoffice records and became one of the highest grossing films in history (save in the UK, where the British Board of Film Classification banned the feature from the video market for 15 years). As Blatty had hoped, the film also prompted a broad cultural debate about the existence of the devil, demons, and fundamentals of religious faith; though no such study has been done, an argument could be made for the role *The Exorcist* played in swelling the ranks of fundamentalist Christianity in subsequent years.

Warner Brothers previously released a 25th Anniversary restoration and re-release on video and DVD in December 1998, which mounted renewed interest in the film. I would argue further that it was British author and film scholar Mark Kemode's dedicated Exorcist research, articles (including an extensive piece in *The Video Watchdog* magazine), book (for the British Film Institute), and UK television documentary (included in its complete form on the 25th Anniversary DVD) that culminated in this newly-revised edition, *The Exorcist: The Version You've Never Seen Before* (given limited theatrical release last summer as *The Exorcist 2000*).

A detailed study of both versions yielded thirteen visual and editing revisions in all, along with the extensive (and altogether very effective) soundtrack remix for digital audio technologies that simply didn't exist in 1973. This new material indeed alters the film's calculated tenor, tempo, and construction, and proves rewarding for its missteps and successes. The anamorphically enhanced transfer (1.78:1) is equal to that of the definitive '25th Anniversary' DVD presentation, though the detailing of the new 5.1 audio mix outstrips the reissue's 5.1 remix with a surprising, sometimes overdone emphasis on rear channel activity. Sadly, the DVD is compromised by Friedkin's sanctimonious, superfluous commentary, which – unlike his useful, revealing talk on the previous disc — too quickly lapses into the director simply describing the action on the screen. Friedkin offers no anecdotes on the performers, production (Friedkin doesn't even mention makeup *maestro* Dick Smith or Mercedes McCambridge's contributions), the revisions, or indeed any fresh perceptions on his film; he instead drones on, quoting dialogue being spoken onscreen and lapsing into pontificating and quoting *Hamlet* during the film's final act. Save us!

Friedkin the director is still a cunning visual storyteller, though, and his revisions are often compelling. Many viewers might overlook the two new shots (one of the Georgetown MacNeil home in which the film is set, and another of the Virgin Mary statue that is later desecrated) now preceding the film's prologue in Iraq, along with the rather clumsy intrusion of further 'subliminal' images of the scary 'Captain Howdy' visage, the sculpted demon Pazuzu face, and even the ghostly face of Father Karras' (Jason Miller) mother glimpsed in the billowing curtains at Regan's window during the climactic moments. More significant and self-evident are entirely new sequences, including Regan's first visit to the doctor's office, Regan's near-legendary 'spider walk' down the stairs (a genuine *frisson* which abruptly ends with a newly-filmed shock closeup), and brief inserts and dialogue between the key players throughout the concluding exorcism sequences.

Most importantly, Friedkin reconstructs two previously-unseen sequences writer-producer Blatty has championed since the film's 1973 opening: a fleeting but crucial dialogue between Karras and Father Merrin (Max Von Sydow) during a lull in the grueling exorcism, and a wry, comforting coda between Lt. Kinderman (Lee J. Cobb) and Father Dyer (played by religious consultant Reverend William J. O'Malley, S.J.). Though it's nice to see the latter, the original film's abrupt ending remains far more powerful; I, for one, do not frequent horror movies seeking succor.

However, viewers troubled by the film's great unanswered *"why"* — why would the Devil choose an innocent little girl as a vehicle for such venomous evil? — will find the new dialogue between Karras and Merrin a revelation. When Karras poses that very question to the titular exorcist, Merrin wearily replies, *"To see ourselves as animal and ugly... to reject the possibility that God could love us."*

The Exorcist remains a powerful film experience, and one well worth experiencing anew in this new version. *(Rated a very strong "R" for strong language, blasphemous imagery and actions, adult and sexual content, violence, and gore.)*[50]

HOLLOW MAN (2000) is the latest science-fiction thriller from Dutch director Paul Verhoeven (*Robocop*, 1987, *Total Recall*, 1990, *Starship Troopers*, 1997, etc.). Though it's essentially a contemporary revamp of H.G.

---

[50] This review was also published in *The Video Watchdog* #71, May 2001, pp. 55-58.

Wells' almost century-old classic novel *The Invisible Man*, its eye-popping visuals owe as much of a debt to the old *"Visible Man"* model kit of the late 1950s. The digital animation and effects work is marvelous throughout, particularly during the film's trio of invisibility reintegration / disintegration sequences engineered by Sony Imageworks' Scott Anderson and a battalion of FX wizards (including Phil Tippett Studios, who previously worked with Verhoeven on *Robocop* and *Starship Troopers*). Watching an adult gorilla and, later, a buff Kevin Bacon stripped down past skin, muscle, organs, and circulatory systems to literal bone is a tough act to top, and this undeniably fantastic work is lovingly detailed in the DVD's ample extras. Alas, if only *Hollow Man*'s script had been given such lavish attention.

This action-horror hybrid chronicles the rise and fall of arrogant scientist Sebastiane Caine (Kevin Bacon), head of a top-secret Pentagon operation seeking to perfect invisibility as a viable weapon. Flush with his current apparent success working with primates, and eager to be the first human being to taste the fruit of his ingenuity, Caine is indeed rendered invisible — but can't reconstitute his form, and begins to edge into sexual predation, megalomania, and homicidal violence. True to the outline and essence of Wells' *Invisible Man* (beautifully filmed in 1933 by director James Whale), *Hollow Man*'s only meaningful expansion on Well's original masterwork addresses Caine's sexual appetite, which is set up via his voyeurism in the opening moments and his ongoing pursuit of his scientific team partner Linda McKay (Elisabeth Shue of *Leaving Las Vegas*, 1995), who rejects the overtures of her former beau Caine to enjoy a more loving relationship with fellow team member Matt Kensington (Josh Brolin).

Thus, the temptations of invisibility invite the narrative's promised confrontation with the sexual politics of the theme — after all, adult preoccupations with invisibility haven't really advanced much beyond the sniggering locker-room fantasies Kevin Bacon admits to in the DVD extras — and Verhoeven was once a filmmaker who would have been up to the challenge. Prior to his Hollywood descent into the lurid flamboyance of (shudder) *Showgirls* (1995), Verhoeven's European films (*Turkish Delight*, 1973; *Keetje Tippel* aka *Katie's Passion*, 1975; *Spetters*, 1980; *The Fourth Man*, 1983) reveled in truly adult explorations of their character's sexuality. Alas, Verhoeven is as much of a team player as his *Hollow Man* characters, and as willing to compromise his vision, derailing the film to bow to studio apprehension and preview audiences' discomfort.

While Andrew Marlowe's script still leads us inexorably from Caine's escalating sexual frustration to voyeurism to predation, the film's final edit cuts a crucial scene in which Caine embraces his condition and appetites to sexually assault a vulnerable neighbor (Rhona Mitra) we've seen him spying on earlier. Though the rape itself could have been handled tastefully or kept offscreen, by building to the event and then cutting it off altogether — and, more importantly, ignoring completely the devastating emotional consequences of Sebastiane's attack — *Hollow Man* cuts out its own black heart. There's no soft-peddling the disturbing, volatile material *Hollow Man* initially engages with: voyeurism, desire, stalking, violation, rape. In fact, prior and contemporary works exploring the invisibility theme have been far more daring (the 1983 film *The Entity*; Italian cartoonist Milo Manara's 1986 graphic novel *Le Parfum de l'Invisible / Butterscotch: The Flavor of the Invisible* and its sequel,[51] Alan Moore and Kevin O'Neill's comics series *The League of Extraordinary Gentlemen*, etc.), leaving *Hollow Man* to its cowardice. Linda's subsequent sexual nightmare (exhibiting her fear of Sebastiane raping her) is a poor substitute, and the film quickly lapses into a vapid final act too reliant on the tried-and-true *Alien* formula.

Flinching from its own subject, the film's second half sadly relegates Sebastiane to being a one-dimensional-monster rampaging through the subterranean military research complex, and echoes the *Alien* and *Aliens* model down to its timed explosions, violent elevator and elevator shaft setpieces, etc. The blood-and-thunder theatrics are further unraveled by the bane of 1990s thrillers, 'multiple false climax' syndrome. While the body count climbs as the cast succumbs to mere head wounds and such, the film's Rasputin-like Sebastiane survives skull-crushing blows, immolation, electrocution, and more to ever-diminishing effect. *Hollow Man* is a hollow movie, and its timidity emphasizes the accomplishment of a film like *The Exorcist*, which lived up to the courage of its convictions and fully engaged with its story, however unsavory the details.

Columbia TriStar's VHS edition, priced for rental, fills the screen quite acceptably, with only a few noticeably cropped compositions. The anamorphically enhanced DVD is letterboxed at 1.85:1, but the real gain is a superb, room-shaking, ear-startling, 5.1 mix. The disc is also quite visibly packed with extras, including a

---

[51] I erroneously identified the Milo Manara erotic invisible man graphic novel as *Clic* in the originally published *Reformer* and *VW* reviews; chalk it up to the danger of writing off the top of one's head without fact-checking…

commentary by Paul Verhoeven, Kevin Bacon and Andrew Marlowe, production notes, HBO's *Making of a Thriller* special, *fifteen* behind-the-scenes featurettes, three deleted scenes viewable with the director's commentary, cast and crew bios, and most collectable of all, an isolated soundtrack channel with commentary by the celebrated composer Jerry Goldsmith. *(Rated "R" for violence, strong language, nudity, adult and sexual content, and gore.)*[52]

January 11:

A note to all avid video renters: Please note that ***The Wonder Boys***, which was originally announced for release this week, has been postponed to make way for another theatrical release. It's too bad, really, since that film would undoubtably have been the pick of the week. In the meantime, there's:

Those of you who bust a gut on the bawdy *There's Something About Mary* (1998), the breakthrough comedy hit from Peter and Bobby Farrelly, will be disappointed by ***ME, MYSELF & IRENE*** (2000), a rather shapeless situational spin on the old *Dr. Jekyll and Mr. Hyde* schtick. Eschewing the 'mad scientist' trappings of other recent *Jekyll & Hyde* revamps (*The Nutty Professor II*) for a juvenile 'Psych 101' approach, the Farrelly Brothers posit that nice-guy human doormat Rhode Island cop Charlie Baileygates (Jim Carrey) harbors a dual persona. Cuckolded by his wife (who sires three robust black homeboy intellectuals Charlie fully accepts and

---

[52] This review was also published in *The Video Watchdog* #70, April 2001, pp. 21-23.

loves as his own), Charlie snaps when she finally leaves him: enter Charlie's surrogate self Hank, a crude lout who vents all of Charlie's buried pain and rage. Both pathological extremes of Charlie/Hank fall for plucky young Irene (Renee Zellweger), whom Charlie is assigned to drive to upper New York State at the behest of a convoluted subplot I won't get into here. Suffice to say a combustible romantic comedy-of-errors ensues, spiced with the Farrelly Brothers' already trademarked blend of lusty and crude antics.

Carrey milks the ridiculous split-persona role for all it's worth, Zellweger is an appealing (and incredibly tolerant) heroine, and the local interest of the Vermont locations (Burlington, Rutland, and elsewhere along Route 7) is an added draw. The devotion and bond between Charlie and his sons is the film's finest invention, and a completely akimbo encounter with a prone Holstein lying in the middle of the road is cruelly funny (leading to one of the film's best pay-off gags in the closing minutes). But the film is a mess, shifting gears with the attention span (but not the pace) of a speed freak; in the end, the needlessly complex villainy is merely discarded with a shrug. Carrey fans, of course, will go for the ride, yawning through the romantic slush and savoring the silliness that does work. *(Rated "R" for strong language, gross-out gags, violence, adult and sexual situations.)*

AUTUMN IN NEW YORK (2000) boasts the silver fox Richard Gere as restauranteur Wil Keane. He's slick in the kitchen and slicker in the bedroom despite his age. It's love at first sight when he meet's an old female friend's daughter (Winona Ryder, as willowy as ever), but, oh, it's terribly sad, because you see, she hasn't long to live...

This May-uh, December romance spin on Erich Segal's venerable *Love Story* (1970) has been given the visual red carpet by director Joan Chen, who should have known better. Elaine Stritch as Ryder's leering grandmother strikes more on-screen sparks than the limp romance manages, but her screen time takes a decided back seat to the seemingly interminable terminal-affair between the limpid duo. Director Chen, a veteran movie and TV (*Twin Peaks*, 1990-91) actress, made her directorial debut in her homeland China with the provocative gem *Xiu Xiu: The Sent Down Girl* (1997), which raised the hackles of the Chinese authorities. Hard to believe the same woman made this treacle. Chalk it up to sophomoric embarrassment, and let's hope her next film re-engages with the passion and vision *Xiu Xiu* unveiled. *(Rated "PG-13" for adult and sexual situations, language.)*

UNDER SUSPICION (2000) is my hands-down pick-of-the-week, brought to a boil by its seasoned leads. This taut, compelling, and truly adult drama set in Puerto Rico quietly pits Morgan Freeman and Gene Hackman against one another in a riveting test of heart and nerves. The arena is the stuffy office of Capt. Victor Benezet (Freeman), who delays the charity speech of old friend and prominent tax attorney Henry Hearst (Hackman) in order to clarify the details of his discovery of a young girl's body. As the clock ticks and Hearst's story unravels, Benezet and hothead Detective Owens (Thomas Jane) turn up the heat as their growing suspicions about the lawyer's possible role in a horrific series of rape-murders of adolescent girls gains momentum. The inevitable conclusions darken as Hearst's estranged wife Chantal (Monica Belluci) is drawn into the investigation, culminating in a genuinely disturbing final act.

Under Suspicion unreels like a perfectly-tuned, self-contained piece of theater. This was an obvious labor of love from Hackman and Freeman, both of whom executive produced the film; they play their roles with exceptional passion and skill, obviously at the peak of their game and reveling in the drama. This is a real gem, relentless and uncompromising in its insidious way. Highly recommended! *(Rated "R" for adult and sexual situations, forensic details, violence, brief nudity, and strong language.)*

January 18:

BATTLEFIELD EARTH: A SAGA OF THE YEAR 3000 (2000): Though *Star Wars* aficionados champion George Lucas' seminal 1977 epic as herald of a new age in sf cinema, history is far enough along to demonstrate quite the opposite. *Star Wars* in fact ushered in a regressive era of heroic and essentially juvenile retro-science-fantasy — and, more dangerously, a sterilized approach to war fiction that reintroduced an equally regressive *"victory culture"* scenario that had been soundly disenfranchised by the grim realities of Cold War paranoia and the Vietnam War. The trend also took a toll on literary sf, and there's no handier landmark of the desolate post-*Star Wars* literary landscape than LaFayette Ron Hubbard's novel *Battlefield Earth: A Saga of the Year 3000* (1982).

Clocking in at an expansive half-a-million words squeezed into 819 pages, *Battlefield Earth* was L. Ron Hubbard's vainglorious return to the field that had nurtured his fame and fortune, *"written to celebrate my fiftieth anniversary as a professional writer."*[53] Hubbard's prolific output for sf pulps of the 1930s and '40s was derailed by the launch of *"Dianetics: The Modern Science of Mental Health"* in the May, 1950 issue of *Astounding* magazine. Within the decade, Dianetics had mutated into Scientology, the religion, and Hubbard was its founder and guru, channeling all his writing efforts into propagandistic literature detailing and promoting his faith.

After almost thirty years away from the field, *Battlefield Earth* was Hubbard's triumphant return to the fold, shamelessly ballyhooed with all the promotional muscle his considerable wealth and power could muster and quickly elevated to best-seller status (over 1.5 million copies sold).

As testosterone-pumped as Robert E. Howard's *Conan* series, shamelessly militaristic as Robert Heinlein's *Starship Troopers* (1959), and blatantly Homeric in scope as Lucas' *Star Wars*, *Battlefield Earth* was essentially an extension of Hubbard's 1940 futuristic war novel *Final Blackout*, supplanting old-fashioned sexist sword'n'sorcery with fancy guns and alien superscience. His hero, Jonnie Goodboy Tyler, was a muscular super-everyman leading an army of almost feral slave-miner Russkies and Scots in their victorious bid to reclaim planet Earth from the tyrannical, materialistic Psychlos, outsized extraterrestrial warlords preprogrammed toward sadism (thanks to *"cruelty fuses"* implanted in their massive skulls) who are themselves subservient to their corporate masters. Premiere Brit sf

---

[53] Hubbard said this in his interview for Charles Platt's *Dream Makers Volume II*, (Berkley Books, 1983), page 186.

author and historian Brian W. Aldiss summed up Bat*tle-field Earth*'s appeal, slant, and paucity of imagination as *"just a simple boy-makes-good story. A bit like Rambo."*[54]

It was indeed a boy's adventure writ large, and among the many readers who fell under its thrall was prominent Hollywood Scientologist John Travolta. By the late 1980s, Travolta's star had fallen to the point where his dream of mounting a multi-million-dollar adaptation of Hubbard's bloated fantasy was a lost cause, but the post-*Pulp Fiction* (1994) resurrection of Travolta's career changed all that. Thus, *Battlefield Earth*, the movie, is now a reality, and a sorrier slice of Millennium-capping sf spam cannot be imagined.

Producer and star Travolta saved the 'choice' role of Psychlo villain Terl for himself, burying himself under pounds of leather costuming, skull-extending dreadlocks, bad dentistry, and rubber monster claws. Playing off his loutish henchman Ker (Forest Whitaker, coasting under similar poundage of dreads, leather, and latex), Travolta is an embarrassment, playing Hubbard's cosmic corporate villainy in the style of Charles Nelson Reilly's '70s-Saturday-morning *Lidsville* buffoonery. Hawk-nosed Barry Pepper (the 1998 *Enemy of the State*'s lead gun-toting cardboard-villain) is equally charmless as Jonnie Goodboy Tyler, snarling his way through his heroic character arc with similarly hawk-nosed Kim Coates as his sidekick Carlo and lovely Sabine Karsenti providing window-dressing as Jonnie's mate Chrissy.

---

[54] Aldiss with David Wingrove, *Trillion Year Spree: The History of Science Fiction* (Atheneum Books/Avon Books, 1986), page 394.

True to Howard/Heinlein/Hubbard heroic sf conventions, the female Chrissy is immediately side-lined, just visible enough to prove Jonnie Boy's heterosexual status before plunging into his sweaty masculine adventure, later used as bait by Terl, and played as a face-sucking trump card once the smoke clears. Like I said, this is a *boy*'s adventure, but unlike a truly engaging boy's adventure like, say, *The 13th Warrior* (1999),[55] *Battlefield Earth* goes through its tired paces without kindling a spark.

The evident efforts of director Roger Christian (recommended to Travolta by none other than George Lucas himself) and Production designer Patrick Tatopoulos (who also designed *Independence Day*, 1996, and *Dark City*, 1998, monster-designer for *Pitch Black*, 2000, and the U.S. remake of *Godzilla*, 1998, etc.) only add to the dung and din; visually, the film is cramped and ugly, and Christian's scheme of keeping the camera perpetually akimbo (as in the recent *Supernova*, 2000[56]) only emphasizes the dank claustrophobia to no good purpose. Christian's credentials are indeed impressive; he's a veteran genre art director (including landmarks like *Alien* and Lucas' *Star Wars* series, where Christian also acted as 2nd Unit director), and he launched his directorial career with the medieval fantasy *Black Angel* (1979) and the still-impressive psychological shocker *The Sender* (1982), but his sf directing efforts thus far have been crippled by lackluster scripts (beginning with *Starship*, 1987).

And make no mistake, *Battlefield Earth* is substandard science-fiction (and fantasy) by any standard, and a

---

[55] See *Blur, Vol. 1*, pp. 185-186.
[56] See *Blur, Vol. 2*, pp. 173-177.

near-mongoloid script in its most rudimentary basics. Having been blasted back into the stone age by the Psychlos (in, we are told, a mere nine minutes), mankind a thousand years hence is living in the realm of Roger Corman's *Teenage Caveman* (a 1958 futuristic sf clinker which was, by the way, a much better movie, awful as it was, and made for a mere fraction of *Battlefield Earth*'s catering budget) — and yet, the phrase "*a piece of cake*" is used throughout. It's a dubious phrase for these dregs of humanity who've never seen, much less tasted, cake in a millennium, and are shown gnashing on raw rats more than once. Later, these virtual cavemen become adept stealth-jet pilots overnight. The Psychlos are supposedly highly-evolved beings, but they come off like a pack of stooges throughout, failing to respond to the increasingly sophisticated behavior of the *"man-animals"* they dismiss as *"rat-brains,"* even after the speed-learning they technologically force-feed Jonnie with has clearly changed the behavior of the entire mongrel pack. Later, when Jonnie substitutes gold bricks stolen from Fort Knox (!) for raw mined ore, Trel accepts the ruse with nary a doubt, having already failed to notice the ludicrous geographical romp Jonnie and his cronies have indulged in (hopping from Colorado to Texas to Kentucky) while supposedly under alien surveillance. Thousand-year-old books are readable and intact, sophisticated high-tech mechanisms are clean and functional, and electricity still flows... ah, what's the point?

Battlefield Earth is an abomination, suitable only for ten-year olds. Sorry, no, that's an insult to kids: even a ten-year-old would see through this tripe. My only recommendation is that, despite the inexplicable PG-13 rating, *Battlefield Earth* is suitable for children, who might indeed enjoy the film for what it is and at its own level. The film is completely chaste (the cartoon villainy renders even the fleeting *"sexual innuendoes"* and brief flicker of an elongated tongue between the Psychlos laughably inoffensive), the violence is utterly bloodless and tastefully off-screen save for the slo-mo demolition of buildings and objects, and the film might serve as a primer to richer sf works kids can savor at a later age. All others, *beware*. This isn't even bad enough to be engaging *as* a bad movie.

Also available as an anamorphically enhanced DVD with audio commentary by director Roger Christian and production designer Patrick Tatopolous, three behind-the-scenes documentaries (*Evolution, Creation* and *Creative Special Effects*), John Travolta's makeup test, storyboards, and some hidden extras. *(Rated "PG-13" for no evident reason I can surmise; this is the cleanest sf movie I've seen in many a year.)*[57]

COYOTE UGLY (2000) is this week's other big new release, and it is as bad as *Battlefield Earth*. No, wait, it's worse. No, really, it is. I can't bring myself to write it up this week; I have to, uh, shovel off my roof instead. No, really, I do. Right now. Tune in next week, same time, same page, and we'll cry in our beer about it.

January 25:

When bar proprietor Lil (Maria Bello) is asked the meaning of the moniker *"Coyote Ugly,"* she replies, *"Did you ever wake up sober after a one-night stand and the person you're next to is laying on your arm, and*

---

[57] This review was also published in *The Video Watchdog* #70, April 2001, pp. 11-13.

they're so ugly you'd rather chew off you arm than risk waking them? That*'s 'Coyote Ugly'"* (and when asked why she named her bar that, she retorts, *"Cheers was taken"*).

There ya go, pardner. That's the cleverest line of dialogue in **COYOTE UGLY** (2000), producer Jerry Bruckheimer's brain-dead revamp of his breakthrough aspiring-ballet-star-welder-by-day-dancer-by-night mega hit *Flashdance* (1983), which was a progressive feminist fable next to this soppy soaper which should have been called *Showgirls Lite*. Perky Piper Perabo stars as whiny Violet Sanford, a New Jersey belle who leaves dad (John Goodman) to seek fame and fortune as a song-writer in the Big Apple. After the usual setbacks — rejection of her demo tapes, her shabby apartment robbed and trashed, and no work — Violet lands at the doorstep of the Coyote Ugly bar, where the oversexed but tomboyish team of bartending *"coyotes"* (Izabelle Miko, Tyra Banks, and Bridget Moynahan) tease the customers with impromptu bar dances, fire walks, and gallons of spilled and sprayed booze.

We're deep in la-la land by this point. Bartenders are fired for spilling less liquid than the coyotes waste in the first thirty seconds of bar screentime here, and it's hard to imagine what portion of the jaded NYC population could be so devoted to a clutch of sassy, obnoxious pseudo-strippers who never strip, really (even a late-in-the-game wet t-shirt frenzy fails to titillate, given the non-revealing colors and costuming).

With Violet's dreams at center stage along with the boisterous female-bonding, the target audience would seem to be young girls, but *Coyote Ugly* was marketed as a slice of titillation more suitable for horny adolescent boys and men. Given the previews, I was confused last summer by the fact that fifteen-year-old boys walked out of this movie until it became apparent halfway through that I had seen far more skin from Violet's Aussie beau (Adam Garcia) than I would ever, ever see of the coyotes themselves; barring the tease factor, the film has precious little else going for it. This fairy tale is hardly the kind of fantasy savvy teens of either gender would buy into for a nanosecond (in fact, I'd worry a bit about those who *do*). That impressionable preteens might swallow the film's non-threatening view of NYC and particularly the bar scene, borderline strip-club, and rampant alcohol abuse *Coyote Ugly* revels in is reason enough for parents to be wary of this otherwise retro-rags-to-riches romance.

Violet's pitiful dilemma — stage fright she believes she has inherited from her mother — is a sham, the characters are appetites and ciphers, and whenever the (urp!) story lags, we're back on the roof of Violet's apartment as she stumbles through another turgid lyric. At one point she murmers, *"The great songs last forever,"* but damn if I can recall a single note of her tunes (for which I am eternally grateful). When Violet began to rhapsodize about *"the first time my mother played 'Bridge Over Troubled Water',"* I suddenly remembered something that needed to be done *immediately* in my kitchen. And if I have to suffer through one more Bruckheimer production flaunting *"I Will Survive"* as its anthem, I will find a way to manufacture designer ashtrays out of sections of Bruckheimer's skull. He must have licensed the rights to that '70s atrocity in perpetuity, and is determined to inflict it upon us at every opportunity. In fact, *"I Will Survive"* has perversely become the anthem of corporate America as it fleeces us all, merrily ramming mass-produced dung like this down our throats. I, for one, would like to roll up the tune forever to ram it where the corporate sun don't shine.[58]

Piper Perabo and her co-stars are beauties, but man oh man, there aren't enough brain cells on screen to make oatmeal. This isn't meant to insult the actresses, who give this drek every ounce of their energy; there's just nothing for them to work with beyond keeping their bodies and mouths in perpetual, meaningless motion. On the DVD extras, director David McNally (who keeps the pace brisk and visuals glossy from stem to stern) claims the coyotes are *"as different* [from one another] *as day from night,"* which is hogwash. The coyotes are as interchangeable as Barbie dolls from beginning to end. On the plus side, affable Adam Garcia as potential suitor Kevin O'Donnell is a likable performer in this, his US debut (his first feature, the Australian *Bootmen,* another rags-to-riches romance wedding *Stomp Out Loud* with *The Full Monty*, hits home video on February 27th). Garcia may give susceptible starry-eyed female viewers something to cling to long after the rest of us have tuned out. *(Rated "PG-13" for its relentless sexual tease, alcohol abuse, sexual innuendoes, and strong language; but there's really no — absolutely NO — nudity, realis-*

---

[58] At a 2001 VSDA (Video Software Dealers of America) New England branch seminar, the organizers had the audacity to blare this fucking song over loudspeakers during the opening session – and *insist* the video retailers in the room (down by almost a quarter from the prior year's gathering) get on their feet and join in. I wasn't the only infuriated attendee to refuse, much to the VSDA organizers' ire. This ill-timed abuse was meant to counterbalance the reaming the independent retailers were suffering from the maladroit consolidation of distribution the studios were conspiring to ram down our collective throats; see *Blur, Vol. 2, "Introduction: Focus."*

tic violence, or anything you could possibly mistake for adult content here.)

Misanthropic L.A. "image consultant" Russ Duritz (Bruce Willis) is the character most in need of his own services in **THE KID** (2000), the latest Walt Disney studio family fantasy. Arrogant, belligerent, egocentric, and utterly insufferable, bachelor Duritz indeed ends up on the receiving end of his ruthless perceptions when confronted by himself at eight years old (Spencer Breslin), compliments of the kinds of perverse miracles this peculiar self-reflective strain of contemporary fantasy depends upon. Pudgy li'l Rusty is caustic Russ' worst nightmare — and he won't go away until the lessons Audrey Wells' derivative script is determined to put across have been hammered home.

This 'inner child' comedy-of-manners from director Jon Turteltaub (*Instinct*, 1999) is painless enough, thanks to a stellar cast (Willis, Lili Tomlin, Emily Mortimer) determined to squeeze all the available juice out of the one-note conceit. Despite a couple of imaginative touches (the mysterious red biplane and Skyway Diner), the scenario ultimately plays Rusty as a matchmaker before shifting gears to confront Russ with the quietly devastating trauma of his youth and wrap up its simplistic pop-psychological profile in tried-and-true fashion. The film is an entry in the introspective 'doppelganger' fantasy that fueled *Passion of Mind* and *Family Man* (both 2000, the latter a gender-reversal of the best of the contemporary lot, *Me, Myself, I*, 1999), but its final fillip posits *The Kid* as a comforting comedic variation on the recent time-twister *Frequency*, which is a much better film in every way. *The Kid* is light and goes down easy, but you'll hate yourself in the morning.

(Rated "PG" for brief strong language and tame 'violence': a car chase placing bicycling Rusty in harm's way.)

February 1:

The recent revival of influential European horror films of the '60s and '70s on video and DVD is worthy of an article in and of itself, but Kino Video's current release of Georges Franju's masterpiece ***LES YEUX SANS VISAGE*** (***EYES WITHOUT A FACE***, 1959) is particularly noteworthy. From its opening title sequence — shot from within a car hurtling through the night to the strains of Maurice Jarre's slippery main theme, its flickering headlights strobbing the splayed bare limbs of the trees overhead as if they were spider webs — Franju's thriller is eerily mesmerizing, fusing an uncanny dreamlike atmosphere with the excesses of the notorious Parisian *Grand Guignol*.

Like fellow French artist and filmmaker Jean Cocteau (who greatly admired this film), Franju infuses even the cruelest passages with genuine poetry. The skeletal narrative is pure *Guignol* (from a novel by Jean Redon, adapted in collaboration with Pierre Boileau and Thomas Narcejac, the authors of *Les Diaboliques*, 1955, and the source novel for Alfred Hitchcock's *Vertigo*, 1958). Aided by his utterly devoted assistant Louise (Alida Valli), celebrated plastic surgeon Dr. Genessier (Pierre Brasseur) is covertly kidnapping young girls to graft their facial features onto the ravaged face of his long-suffering daughter Christiane (Edith Scob). Though forty years on and filmed in black and white (by master cinematographer Eugen Shuftan), Franju's horrors still pack a punch — particularly in Kino's uncut print, which restores footage never before seen in America — in part because of the sterile quiet they occur within. The film's most infamous passage details Genessier's transplant procedure with ruthless clarity, shrouded in a silence pierced only by the cold ring of surgical instruments, the soft rustle of clothing, and the occasional offscreen barking of Genessier's caged dogs.

Unnerving as the overt mayhem remains, it's the austere allure of the film that lingers, embodied by Edith Scob's unforgettable performance beneath the porcelain mask that hides her disfigurement. Christiane is a truly tragic figure, and Franju and Scob engrave her plight into our hearts. In a film brimming with indelible images, Scob's pantomime and iconic beauty haunts its most memorable moments: accepting Louise's strange, almost canine affection as her hair is brushed; gliding down the stairs and into the operation chamber to contemplate her father's handiwork; gingerly cradling the phone receiver to call her fiance (who believes she is dead) and whisper his name; pausing to accept a "kiss" from her father's tortured dogs as she frees them from their pens, her hair stirred by the freed white doves that flit around her head.

Franju remains a sadly neglected filmmaker in his own country and an unknown here. This, his second feature, received a cursory 1962 theatrical release in the U.S., badly dubbed and hideously retitled *The Horror Chamber of Dr. Faustus* to play grindhouses on a double-bill with the US/Japanese two-headed-man shocker *The Manster*. Though critics Pauline Kael and Raymond Durgnat sang its praises, the film was ignored and almost immediately exiled (and cut further) to rare showings on late night television. A proper revival of *Eyes Without a Face* is long overdue.

Thankfully, Kino has restored subtitled version is exquisite, a vast improvement over 'gray-market' bootlegs and an earlier Interama Inc. video release. Though has yet to issue the film on DVD, it certainly deserves the added luster such a showcase would bring (coupled, perhaps, with Franju's seminal 1949 short film *Le Sang des Bêtes/Blood of the Beasts*).[59]

Countless suspense and horror films have pirated *Eyes Without a Face*, from Jess Franco's *The Awful Dr. Orloff* (*Gritos en la Noche*, 1962) to Clive Barker's *Hellraiser* (1987) to John Woo's *Face/Off* (1998). None have matched the power of Franju's ravishing, glacial nightmare. This is a classic, not to be missed! *(Made almost a decade before the MPAA ratings system,* Eyes Without a Face *is unrated, but it most likely would be rated 'PG-13' or a soft 'R' for its theme, gore, violence, and mild suggested sexuality.)*

The derivative thriller **WHAT LIES BENEATH** (2000) should have been entitled *What Lies Between*, filmed by director Robert Zemeckis as the *Cast Away* shoot broke for Tom Hanks' crash-course weight-loss program. Zemeckis is a nimble enough mainstream director (the *Back to the Future* series, 1985-90, *Forrest Gump*, 1994, *Contact*, 1997), but this lazy exercise is a time-killer at best. It rips Hitchcock's *Rear Window* (1954; did the neighbor kill his wife?) before pirating its second act from much-better ghost movies (*A Stir of Echoes*, 1999), culminating in a contrived bathroom set-

---

[59] The Criterion Collection released *Les Yeux Sans Visage* on DVD in October, 2004 – with *Le Sang des Bete* and many other extras, including rare makeup shots from *Les Yeux* from my own collection.

piece in which hopes to do for tubs what *Psycho* did for showers. Don't worry, draw a bath. The crazy-quilt script implodes into a shrill *"triple-twist, double-whammy"* finale and the fakest CGI cemetery ever seen. Worse still, the preview (as contemporary Hollywood previews tend to do) gives away every plot point, a practice Zemeckis condones; proof, if any more were needed, of how little regard Zemeckis has for his target audience. Filmed in Vermont, though there isn't a single Vermont-like being in sight, even as window dressing. Thankfully, Michelle Pfeiffer enlivens the creaky blood & thunder with a genuine performance and remains the film's greatest virtue. *(Rated 'PG-13' for language, violence — ah, it doesn't matter, nothing here to upset or offend, really.)*

The first wordless theatrical preview for Disney Studios' CGI-epic **DINOSAUR** (2000) had audiences gasping at its vivid panorama of prehistoric life; they groaned at the second, which revealed the dinosaurs (and primate sidekicks) talked. Thankfully, they don't sing. Disney's *Dinosaur* boasts a reported $200 million budget and ballyhoos itself as *"the most technologically advanced film ever"* (meaning – *what?*), but squanders it on talkative saurians and an embarrassingly formulaic story.

The visuals are marvelous, the plot is a tired retread of Don Bluth's *The Land Before Time* (1988). I kid you not: a misfit band of herbivores trek across barren wastelands in search of a fabled green valley, stalked by hungry carnivores. Alas, that's what Disney Studio distilled from an original screenplay by Walon Green (*The Wild Bunch*, 1969, etc.) once wed to the *Robocop/Starship Troopers* team of director Paul Verhoeven and special effects wizard Phil Tippett. The result is lovely to look at but utterly toothless (very young tots may find the tame dino mayhem too vivid). Still, there's no denying the consumate skill of the artists who breathe life into the creatures onscreen. See *Dinosaur* (the DVD is splendid) — but don't miss BBC's *Walking With Dinosaurs* mini-series (also on VHS and a stellar DVD), which was everything this could and should have been. *(Rated 'G', suitable for all ages.)*

February 8:

CECIL B. DeMENTED (2000): Inspired by an 'anti-Hollywood' rant published in *Film Threat*, this savage, slapdash satire of the indy filmmaking scene and reality TV opens with an attack on the debut of the latest schmaltzy Hollywood opus from star Honey Whitlock (Melanie Griffith). The target is Honey herself, kidnapped by a mangy pack of ciné-terrorists led by arrogant *auteur* Cecil B. DeMented (Stephen Dorff), who's decided it's high time for Honey's indoctrination to the true path of guerilla cinema, top-lining his latest feature whether she wants to or not. Having sworn himself and his acolytes 'The Sprocket Holes' to a vow of *"celibacy for cinema"* (*"we're horny, but our film comes first!"*), the brainwashing begins with skirmishes against duplex theaters showing films they despise ("Patch Adams *doesn't deserve a Director's Cut — the first one was long enough!"*) and the set of *Gump Again*, the sequel to *Forrest Gump*. The escalating mayhem culminates in a showdown with authorities at the local drive-in, where Cecil, Honey, and the Sprockets hang up their speakers in a blaze of glory.

This is the 15th film (11th feature) from Baltimore-based cult director John Waters (*Pink Flamingos*, 1972, *Hairspray*, 1988, *Cry-Baby*, 1990, etc.), and admittedly among his weaker recent efforts, though there are some hilarious highpoints. The cast revel in their outing with Waters: Dorff plays Cecil's dementia straight, Griffith plunges into Honey's transformation with glee (her final scene, played to Liberace's maudlin *"Ciao!"*, plunges into *Sunset Boulevard* bathos), and the Sprocket Holes (including Adrian Grenier, Alicia Witt, Jack Noseworthy, Mike Shannon, and others) are perfect. Waters' regulars — from onscreen fixtures like Mink Stole and Patricia Hearst (who adds a suitably creepy resonance to the film's concept) to constant collaborators behind the scenes — provide excellent support, but Waters' essential return (some would call it a relapse) to the manic, patchwork energy of his fledgling midnight movies (*Multiple Maniacs*, 1970, *Female Trouble*, 1974, *Desperate Living*, 1977, etc.) will daze the uninitiated. The script is a mess. I'm sure Waters meant Cecil's inability to really make a movie — much less a 'good' movie — part of the gag, the fact that the kamikaze climax revolves around the filming of their final scene instead of the debut of Cecil's *"masterpiece"* short-shrifts the entire premise, as if the commitment to editing and completing a film were beneath concern.

The slyest jokes target cinéastes: a marquee in the opening titles announces that the beloved 1944 French classic *Children of Paradise* is *"Finally Dubbed in English!"* and the director names tattooed on the Sprockets' skins cover all the cult bases. The broader strokes of black comedy are fun, too, as in Mink Stole's caustic exchanges with an angry, unwilling kid (Jeffrey Wei) forced to participate in the Hollywood debut fundraiser (a *Jerry's Telethon* nightmare, and closer to the vein most Waters fans enjoy). I enjoyed *Cecil B. DeMented* on its own terms much more the second time around, after initial expectations (I try not to approach *any* film with expectations) had been dashed. Waters' lively commentary track is the icing on the DVD cake. A self-confessed *"chatty Kathy,"* Waters' comments are riotous, 'dishing' on the cast (those whiskers on Harriet Dodge are the real thing!), behind-the-scenes 'dirt', and very funny asides about the director's pet peeves, some of which you'll probably share. *(Rated 'R' for all manner of despicable sociopathic behavior, including violence, gunplay, drug abuse, nudity, etc.)*[60]

DR. T & THE WOMEN (2000), the latest from eclectic director Robert Altman (*M*A*S*H*, 1970, *McCabe & Mrs. Miller*, 1971, *Nashville*, 1975, *The Player*, 1992, *Short Cuts*, 1993, etc.), offers Richard Gere his best showcase in years, surrounding him with a veritable tsunami of top-drawer actresses. The title sequence in Dr. T's crowded gynecology office is a succinct snapshot of Altman's trademark style: the layered dialogue grows denser as the frame fills with chattering women, building to a deafening cacophony. Gross as the caricature seems, the performers savor every morsel of screen time and scenery in chewing range, improvising to jazzmeister Altman's lead.

Gere is the titular 'Dr. T' — Dr. Sullivan Travis, OB-GYN — much in demand among the female aristocracy of Dallas. Like a sailor adrift, Travis is plagued by *"water, water, everywhere, but not a drop to drink."* He

---

[60] This review was also published in *Video Watchdog* #81, March 2002, pp. 10-11.

sees to his patients' every need, but aches for emotional intimacy. His wife Kate (Farrah Fawcett) rejects his slightest touch, spiraling into a breakdown; the shallow narcissism of his daughters (Tara Reid and Kate Hudson) and intrusion of his meddling sister-in-law (Laura Dern) only hastens the good doctor's pursuit of golf instructor Bree (Helen Hunt), a novelty in Dr. T's existence precisely since she doesn't need him. As in the title sequence, the background static swells in volume and urgency until it overwhelms Travis in the finale's eruption of marriage complications, personal revelations, and a wild and woolly 'Act of God'.

Some may be put off by Altman's take on all things female and Texan, though the screenplay is by Ann Rapp and the predominately female cast engage with all cylinders firing. Edweena Twilley (aka Mary-Lou Truelove), a true-blue born-and-bred Texan co-worker at First Run Video, assures me that *Dr. T*'s seemingly-extreme portraits of Dallas womanhood and weather are *absolutely* on-the-money. The stellar cast and Lyle Lovett's seductive score are the glue that holds Rapp and Altman's rambling shaggy-dog tale together. *Dr. T* is a 'love-it-or-leave-it' concoction, closest in tenor, tone, and plot particulars to Altman's *A Wedding* (1978), a film most critics and audiences despised, but which I quite inexpicably liked... as I did *Dr. T & The Women*. The doctor will see you now... *(Rated 'R' for nudity, strong language, adult and sexual content, and discreetly-filmed gynecological examinations.)*

February 15:

The 265 minute, two-tape video release and two-disc DVD debut of the ***DUNE*** (2000) mini-series remake isn't an expanded version of David Lynch's infamous 1984 theatrical adaptation of Frank Herbert's science fiction classic.[61] It's Sci-Fi Channel's December, 2000 mini-series (originally broadcast over three nights, December 3-5), now available *sans* distracting commercials — and it's one of the best science fiction adaptations ever. Unlike Lynch's visually rich but hopelessly muddled adaptation, the remake's expanded running time allows for a far more coherent devotion to its source, one of the finest sf novels ever written. Despite the relative modesty of its means alongside the multi-millions lavished on fattened juggernauts like *Battlefield Earth* and the equally odious *Star Wars: Episode 1: The Phantom Menace*, writer/director John Harrison's made-for-TV adaptation is earnest, ambitious, and truly marvelous sf of substance and depth. As made-for-TV science fiction, it ranks alongside landmarks like the Nigel Kneale *Quatermass* originals (1953-1979), or the PBS adaptation of Ursula LeGuin's *The Lathe of Heaven* (1980),[62] instead of joining the ranks of misbegotten past efforts at adapting classic sf to the small screen, as in Michael Anderson's wretched NBC miniseries adaptation of Ray Bradbury's *The Martian Chronicles* (1979).

True to the letter and spirit of Frank Herbert's ecological and political epic, Harrison's *Dune* details the tyrannical suppression and subsequent eruption of a planetary Jihad that literally shakes the cosmos. The

---

[61] Make no mistake: I love Lynch's *Dune*, in all its incarnations (theatrical version and the expanded edition Lynch disowns) – but it was and remains a deeply flawed work, and fails as an adaptation of Herbert's novel.

[62] See *Blur, Vol. 2*, pp. 199-203. Note that *Lathe of Heaven* was remade, again for TV, in 2002.

feuding houses of noble Atreides and the corrupt Harkonnon are pitched against one another on the barren desert planet Dune, source of the all-important 'spice' necessary to all space travel. A covert plot against the Atreides drives the surviving heir Paul (Alec Newman) and his mother Jessica (Saskia Reeves) into the wasteland. The Harkonnons assume mother and son are dead; they are, in fact, alive and taken in by the nomadic tribal people known as the Fremen, who alone grasp the unique relation between 'the spice' and the fragile ecosystem dominated by gigantic sandworms. As Paul matures, assuming a messianic role predestined among the Fremen, his relation to all around him irrevocably alters, culminating in all-out war with the fate of 'spice' production — and thus, the universe — falling firmly into his grasp.

This review does not afford the attention this film deserves. Though hardly opulent (the desert and war scenes are sometimes stagebound, and Ernest Farino's economic CGI-effects work fall short of the grand scale the tale deserves), Harrison's *Dune* carefully orchestrates its dramatic and visual resources for maximum effect. A pragmatic budgetary decision to eschew the costly delays of filming in an actual desert local (the African Namibia desert was scouted) to embrace a four-month shoot in controllable studio environments in the Czech Republic could have been fatal to the production, but innovative techniques conceived and executed by celebrated cinematographer Vittorio Storaro (*Apocalypse Now*, 1979, *Reds*, 1981, *The Last Emperor*, 1987, *The Sheltering Sky*, 1990, *Little Buddha*, 1993, etc.) create an evocative variety of believable exteriors and desert locales along with the lavish palace, chamber, and cavern interiors. Storaro's efforts add immeasurably to the production and emotional tapestry, and offer a textbook example of visionary (and veteran) ingenuity overcoming budgetary restrictions.

Equally important, the interior landscapes of character and story are believably conveyed: writer/director Harrison admirably captures the individuals, court intrigue, and mythic resonance of Herbert's parable. My initial reservations about star Alec Newman (a Glasgow born, London-raised performer who seems, at first, a wan Keir Dullea lookalike) crumbled as he grows into the role of Paul; he is, in the end, marvelous. In fact, the entire cast is striking, though I miss the tactile vileness of David Lynch's Baron Harkonnen (Kenneth McMillan), played here in appropriate *I, Claudius* fashion by Ian McNeice.

Comparisons to Lynch's theatrical feature are unavoidable, and part of the fascination. As a director, Harrison — a veteran of Rubenstein's stable since the *Tales from the Darkside* TV series (1984-88) and theatrical omnibus feature, most recently helmed cable movies like *Donor Unknown* (1995) and *The Assassination File* (1996), and scripted the Disney CGI *Dinosaur* (2000) — is a far more linear (and thus, coherent) storyteller than Lynch, but never as cinematically adventurous. At its best, Lynch's *Dune* creates an uncanny atmosphere and truly dreamlike environment; at its best, Harrison's *Dune* vividly inhabits and relates its epic story with sometimes startling clarity. Hence, the mysticism and importance of dreams shape Lynch's *Dune*; no surprise, then, that the religious order of the Bene Gesserit sisterhood carries a stronger presence in the Lynch version, as do the Mentats and the Guild, while the multi-layered familial and court intrigue is more fully realized in Harrison's adaptation. Harrison also plays down the violence of his adaptation, and never approaches the *grand guignol* excesses of Lynch's version (such as Baron Harkonnen's gross condition and appetites, including the gruesome quasi-rape of a young acolyte). As admirable, visionary and personal as Lynch's interpretation is, Harrison's is unquestionably the superior translation of Herbert's novel to film.

For instance, one of the great flaws of Lynch's adaptation lay in the fizzled climactic showdown between Lynch's Paul (Kyle MacLachlan) and Feyd Harkonnen (Sting); since we have witnessed Paul's growth as a warrior, and seen Feyd only strut and pose like a rooster, there was no sense of Feyd being a threat to Paul, no sense of danger to fuel the duel. Harrison carefully delineates his Feyd (Matt Keeslar of *Safe Passage*, 1994, *Scream 3*, 2000, etc.) as a ruthless and prolific killer (celebrating, at one point, his one-hundredth kill) willing to 'cheat' to succeed (demonstrated by his failed assassination attempt on his father). This lends the climactic confrontation between Paul and Feyd a suspense and electricity Lynch was incapable of generating (Lynch is hardly alone in this failing; a similar lack of simple narrative attention hamstrung the climactic duel of George Lucas' *Star Wars Episode I: The Phantom Menace*, 1999).

Though Harrison's cast is excellent, they are less striking than Lynch's stellar cast. Supporting characters like Thufir Hawat, Gurney Halleck, the Shadout Mapes, and Dr. Kynes were more memorable in Lynch's version, however slight their screen time, due to the iconic stature of the actors playing those roles (played, respectively, by Freddie Jones, Patrick Stewart, Linda Hunt, and Max Von Sydow). That said, Harrison's characterizations are much, much richer, thanks in part to the generous running time he has to work with. Harrison's rendition of the Emperor (Giancarlo Giannini) and his daughter, the Princess Irulan (Julie Cox, beautifully playing a character who was barely a cipher in Lynch's adaptation), add immeasurably to the film. Among the many strengths of Harrison's adaptation is the always compelling delineation of the political and court intrigues, and the various cultures (primarily the Fremen culture); the bond between father (Leto) and son (Paul) is strongly conveyed and maintained throughout; Paul's character arc and transformation is fully developed, embracing his growing Messianic megalomania which plants the seed for the direction of Herbert's subsequent *Dune* novels; and Harrison succinctly conveys the all-important relationship between the worms and the spice, the heart of the ecology of Arrakis (and, thus, the novel), a vital plot-point that was hopelessly lost in Lynch's adaptation.

On the other hand, the Harrison adaptation completely fudges the betrayal of the House Atreides. The key character of Dr. Yueh (played here by Robert Russell) is poorly established, and the crucial element of the poisonous tooth Yeuh implants into the mouth of Duke Leto (William Hurt) is so dimly communicated as a story point that it's possible to watch the sequence unfold with absolutely no idea of what is going on. In Lynch's film, Yueh (Dean Stockwell) is vividly delineated with minimal screentime; the insertion of the tooth into the jaws of Duke Leto (Jurgen Prochnow) rendered with painful immediacy, the import of the tooth stressed with the same deft shorthand Lynch lends all the omens that inhabit the film, and Leto's failed dying attempt to use the tooth to kill the Baron Harkonnen punctuated by the staging and Kenneth McMillan's over-the-top playing of the Baron's relief at still being alive. This lapse is hardly characteristic of Harrison's fine work, though; indeed, the narrative quickly recovers from this misstep, and never strays or stumbles thereafter, which certainly cannot be said for the Lynch version, in which such lucid storytelling was the exception, not the rule.

Other arguable detriments of the Harrison version include the sketchy depiction of Paul and Jessica's abandonment to the desert; the reinterpretation of 'The Weirding Way' as a martial art, vaguely introduced in the 2nd chapter (Lynch's interpretation, in which concentrated use of sound waves is magnified to lethal proportions, was set up in its first act and a more cohesive element of the whole), though it is adequately developed for the final act; and the decision to eschew the novelistic device of sharing the characters' internal thoughts with the audience (presented as voiceovers in the Lynch adaptation) takes a toll on the early portions of the film, in which crucial elements (e.g., the Bene Gesserit religion and particularly their use of 'The Voice') are left unexplained. Harrison quickly makes this decision a narrative strength, but the difficulties of translating many of Herbert's vital imaginative concepts to a linear visual telling of the tale must be acknowledged.

Both versions of *Dune* fail to convincingly portray Herbert's most *outré* conceits: Ernest Farino's worms are ultimately more satisfying than the clumsy constructs special effects creator Carlo Rambaldi fashioned for Lynch's adaptation, though both fall far short of the majestic creatures Herbert envisioned — nor do they hold a candle to the unsettlingly alive creations that burrowed through Ron Underwood's *Tremors* (1989). The riding of the worms is risible in both versions, though Harrison's staging is a slight improvement on Lynch's inadvertantly hilarious parallel sequence. Lynch and Rambaldi's almost fetal Guild Navigators were more compelling and disturbing creatures than Farino's pseudo-winged (with skin stretched between spidery fingers, like a bat's wing) amphibian-like Navigators, but neither film adequately depicts the Navigators' abilities to *"fold space,"* the transportation method central to Herbert's invented universe and the reason the spice is so vital to it.

That said, Farino and his collaborators work wonders with the budget and time restraints they labored within, and this Watchdog has a fondness for seeing Farino's growing credits in the field. In his youth, Farino was the founder/publisher/editor of the extraordinary Ray Harryhausen fanzine *FXRH* (which I faithfully subscribed to), a precursor to subsequent books and zines (and, given its devotion to excavating the minutae of Harryhausen lore and 'lost footage,' a forefather of the *Video Watchdog* in its way). It's been exciting to see Farino work in the very field he devoted his fan activities to, racking up some pretty impressive credentials (e.g., *Galaxy of Terror*, 1981, *The Terminator*, 1984, and *Terminator 2: Judgment Day*, 1991, *The Abyss*, 1989, *Screamers*, 1995, and the recent Tom Hanks' mini-series *From the Earth to the Moon*, 1998) and even stretching his skills with the occasional directing stint (e.g., four episodes of the TV series *Monsters*, 1989-91, and the *Land of the Lost* revival, 1991, features *Steel and Lace*, 1990, and Chapter 1 and 5 of Charles Band's *Josh Kirby... Time Warrior* direct-to-video series, 1995-96). Overall, Farino's work in *Dune* is excellent, orchestrating a fairly seamless vision from a blend of live-action effects, miniatures, and CGI.

As usual, the two-disc DVD set boasts the prefered transfer. Warner Advanced Media Operations (WAMO) handsome menu designs, compression, encoding, and authoring are excellent, and each episode is well-chaptered. The first disc features Episode One, *"Arrakis"* (clocking in at 89m 29s), in 19 chapters, and Episode Two, *"Muad'dib"* (87m 36s), is divided into a more generous 23 chapters. Disc Two offers Episode Three, *"The Prophet"* (89m 17s), is presented in 24 chapters, accompanied by the *"Special Features"* extras (a *"Special Features"* menu option on Disc 1 simply refers one to Disc 2). These extras include a short documentary on the making of the film, *"Frank Herbert's Dune: The Lure of Spice"* (25m 39s), two galleries (Costume Design and Production Design), and a text piece, *"Dune: A Cinematographic Treatment,"* by cinematographer Vittorio Stararo. All in all, not counting the time one may take stepping through the two galleries and reading Storaro's remarkable aesthetic dissection of his chromatic and elemental approach to the film, the DVD set offers four hours, 51 minutes, and 57 seconds of material, and is clearly a bargain at Artisan's sell-through pricing.

While *Dune*'s DVD extras are outstanding, they nevertheless fall far short of a prior DVD presentation that was included in copies of a book still available in bookstores and via online sources, *The Secrets of Frank Herbert's Dune* by James Van Hise.[63] The book itself is

---

[63] This book was a collaboration of ibooks and New Amsterdam Entertainment, distributed by Simon & Schuster (2000, 160 pages, ISBN #0-7434-0730-X). At the time of this writing, used copies were still available online at incredibly low prices; just be sure the DVD is in the copy of the book you're

a perfectly adequate and lavishly illustrated overview of the production, offering the complete text of Vittorio Storaro's treatise its the final chapter,[64] but the Region 1 DVD packaged along with the book is a marvel that eclipses the relative paucity of supplements on the official DVD release. In fact, the official DVD 'making of' featurette, *"The Lure of Spice,"* is a 25-minute condensation of the far more abundant background material included on the book's DVD, which clocks in at a feature-length *79m 5s!*

The Secrets of Frank Herbert's Dune (book DVD) offers 8 chapters of material, most featuring a 'mini-movie' featurette plus seperate 'Design and Sketches' and 'Still Photo' galleries which are accessible seperately or as part of a complete play-through of the entire disc. These are: the introductory *"In the Beginnning..."* (7m 25s); *"Cast and Characters"* (17m 1s, accessible via 11 chapter stops) plus gallery (8m 12s); *"Production Design"* (7m 4s) plus gallery (5:47); *"Costume Design"* (2:55) plus gallery (4m 52s); *"Special, Mechanical, and Visual Effects"* (four chapter stops, cumulatively totalling 6m 58s) plus gallery (4m 7s); *"Cinematography"* (5m 6s) plus gallery (2m 42s); the gallery-format *"'Family' Snapshot Album"* (5m 21s); and *"DVD Credits"* (58s) plus the original Sci-Fi Channel trailor for the mini-series (37s) and a weblink to Sci-Fi Channel's *Dune* site (for compatible DVD-Rom drives).

---

buying. See http://www.amazon.com/Secrets-Frank-HerbertS-Dune/dp/074340730X/ref=sr_1_1?ie=UTF8&s=books&qid=1217876759&sr=8-1 and http://www.abebooks.com/servlet/SearchResults?an=James+Van+Hise&sts=t&tn=The+Secrets+of+Frank+Herbert%27s+Dune&x=47&y=8

[64] *"Cinematography Ideation of the Film,"* pages 146-153.

Artisan's official DVD release extra, *"The Lure of Spice,"* offers single interview bytes from each cast member, along with similar excerpt bytes from key production personel, all boiled down from the book's DVD. Artisan's extras are weak tea compared to the rich selection of interview source material in *The Secrets of...*, which generously intercuts the cast and crews comments about their collaborative efforts with each portrait of those respective jobs. The *Secrets* DVD was produced and mastered by Zuma Digital, with editorial and post-production services provided by Lumina Films, Ltd.; WAMO's transfer of the condensed version does refine the audio track a bit (less ambient noise and 'tin'), but such fine-tuning pales alongside the relative paucity of material *"The Lure of Spice"* offers. Passionate *Dune* fans will find *The Secrets of Frank Herbert's Dune* book and accompanying DVD a necessary addition to their library, and a welcome accessory to Artisan's otherwise sterling DVD.[65]

An aside to *Star Wars* junkies: don't mistake the similarities between *Dune* and George Lucas' celebrated series as evidence of *Dune* having 'ripped off' *Star Wars*. Quite the opposite: Herbert's novel pre-dated *Star Wars* by over a decade.[66] May any of you who suggest otherwise be fed to a sandworm for your ignorance.

---

[65] James Van Hise's book is also a nifty companion to the long out-of-print paperback on David Lynch's feature, *The Making of Dune* by Ed Naha (Berkley Books, 1984, 301 pages, ISBN # 0-425-07376-9), also recommended for *Dune* and David Lynch fans.

[66] The same goes for Hayao Miyazaki fans: Miyazaki's sole graphic novel *Nausicaä of the Valley of the Wind/Kaze no tani no Naushika* (1982-1994) and 1984 anime feature adaptation are marvelous, but both owe a huge debt to *Dune*.

Whether you embrace *Dune* on video or DVD, this fine film earns my highest recommendation. *(Though* Dune *is unrated, it would most likely earn a 'PG-13'; the warfare violence is tastefully handled, as are the adult and sexual themes — including a discreetly staged Fremen bacchanal — but parental guidance is suggested.)* [67]

* ***DUNE***: This 265 minute, two-tape set isn't an expanded version of David Lynch's infamous 1984 theatrical adaptation of Frank Herbert's science fiction classic. It's Sci-Fi Channel's brand-new mini-series, now available sans distracting commercials — and it's one of the best science fiction films ever made. Unlike Lynch's visually rich but hopelessly muddled adaptation, the remake's expanded running time allows for a far more coherent devotion to its source, one of the finest sf novels ever written. Despite the relative modesty of its means alongside the multi-millions lavished on fattened juggernauts like *Battlefield Earth* and the equally odious *Star Wars Episode 1: The Phantom Menace*, writer/director John Harrison's made-for-TV adaptation is earnest, ambitious, and truly marvelous sf of substance and depth.

True to the letter and spirit of Frank Herbert's ecological and political epic, *Dune* details the tyrannical suppression and subsequent eruption of a planetary Jihad that literally shakes the cosmos. The feuding houses of noble Atreides and the corrupt Harkonnon are pitched against one another on the barren desert planet Dune, source of the all-important "spice" necessary to all space travel. A covert plot against the Atreides drives the surviving heir Paul (Alec Newman) and his mother Jessica

---

[67] A slightly abridged version of this complete essay was the cover feature in *Video Watchdog* #72, June 2001, pp. 36-41.

(Saskia Reeves) into the wasteland. The Harkonnons assume mother and son are dead; they are, in fact, alive and taken in by the nomadic tribal people known as the Fremen, who alone grasp the unique relation between 'the spice' and the fragile ecosystem dominated by gigantic sandworms. As Paul matures, assuming a messianic role predestined among the Fremen, his relation to all around him irrevocably alters, culminating in all-out war with the fate of 'spice' production — and thus, the universe — falling firmly into his grasp.

This column does not afford the attention this film deserves. Though hardly opulent (the desert and war scenes are sometimes stagebound, and Ernest Farino's economic CGI-effects work fall short of the grand scale the tale deserves), this version of *Dune* carefully orchestrates its dramatic and visual resources for maximum effect. Harrison admirably captures the characters, court intrigue, and mythic resonance of Herbert's parable. My initial reservations about star Alec Newman (who seems, at first, a wan Keir Dullea lookalike) crumbled as he grows into the role of Paul; in fact, the entire cast is striking (though I miss the over-the-top vileness of David Lynch's Baron Harkonnon, played here in *I, Claudius* fashion by Ian McNeice).

An aside to *Star Wars* junkies: don't mistake the similarities between *Dune* and George Lucas' celebrated series as *Dune* having 'ripped off' *Star Wars*. Quite the opposite: Herbert's novel pre-dated *Star Wars* by over a decade. May any of you who suggest otherwise be fed to a sandworm for your ignorance. DVD lovers note: the DVD release of *Dune* is slated for March. It's reportedly packed with juicy extras, and the clarity of presentation alone guarentees a worthwhile rental or purchase. Whether you wait for the DVD or jump into the VHS version currently available, this fine film earns my highest recommendation. *(Though* Dune *is unrated, it would most likely earn a 'PG-13'; the warfare violence is tastefully handled, as are the adult and sexual themes — including a discreetly staged Fremen bacchanal — but parental guidance is suggested.)*[68]

URBAN LEGENDS: FINAL CUT (2000): I don't ask much of bad horror movies. Just keep the twisted 10-year-old in me happy and I'm there. Recent direct-to-vid monstrosities like *Crocodile, Python*, and *Spiders* are saddled with derivative scripts, vacuous characters, and impoverished budgets, but they're honest and entertaining in their way. The era of CGI effects affords *Crocodile* (directed by slumming Tobe Hooper of 1974's *The Texas Chainsaw Massacre* infamy) and even an 18-day wonder like *Python* (from the one-note author of *Anaconda*!) some eye-popping setpieces as the titular reptiles swallow the hapless cast; *Spiders* gleefully spices its fusion of retro-1950s-web-slinging and post-*Alien* mayhem with splashy grue and outlandish arachnid action. It's dumb as a bag of hammers, but it's also the liveliest (mind you, not the best) giant spider movie ever made.

Alas, this unnecessary sequel to the vapid *Urban Legends* (1998) doesn't approach the cheap thrills of a *Spiders* or *Python*, much less *Scream* (1996), the surprise hit that triggered the current teen-body-count slasher cycle. *Urban Legends: Final Cut* (we can only hope!) sucks like a bucket of ticks, failing even to live down to the first *Urban Legends*. It eschews the premise

---

[68] This is the edit of the *Dune* review that was published in *The Brattleboro Reformer*.

of a killer recreating popular 'urban legends'; the only tenuous link is the return of security-guard Reece (Loretta Divine) and a coda cameo by another original cast member. Instead, eyes glaze and pulses slow as a masked killer decimates a film school, inviting all manner of amateurish 'homages' to Alfred Hitchcock which emphasize the utter paucity of suspense. Adding insult to injury, the sole dollop of gore — a Dario Argento-esque decapitation — was obviously inserted *after* the producers realized the film needed something to break the monotony or justify the 'R' rating. The 'deleted scenes' among the DVD extras (sure to raise gorehound expectations) offer only more empty-headed exposition. This offal was the single worst film I subjected myself to last year in any media... and believe you me, I sat through some real porkers. You've been duly warned!

At the time of writing, *Urban Legends: Final Cut* is priced only for rental on VHS, but believe it or not, there's also a DVD. Even harder to believe, it's presented in an anamorphic transfer, with an audio commentary by the director (John Ottman), a 'making of' documentary, theatrical trailers, deleted scenes, even a gag reel. No comment.[69]

On the other hand, *do* rent the 'sleeper' **CHERRY FALLS** (2000), which beats every single sequel in the *Scream/I Know What You Did Last Summer/Urban Legends* franchises at their own game. The premise is rudimentary — a small town is ravaged by a psycho killer targeting virgins — but it toys with the cliches of the

---

[69] An adapted version of this review was also published in *The Video Watchdog* #70, April 2001, pg. 27, and in *VMag* #39, March 2001, pg. 28.

'teen slasher' genre with a certain wit and style. Michael Biehn (*The Abyss,* 1989, *Aliens,* 1986, etc., who debuted on the big screen in *Coach,* 1978, and in horror films as the obsessed killer in the semi-slasher *The Fan,* 1981) stars as the town sheriff whose concern for the welfare of his daughter (Brittany Murphy of Clueless) has him praying she's *not* a virgin (a subversive appropriation from *Andy Warhol's Dracula,* aka *Blood for Dracula,* 1974, in which Drac could only drink virgin blood, prompting Joe Dellasandro to deflower all in reach). The rest of the town teens address the situation with a party bacchanal that sets the stage for the grisly climax. The film keeps kicking the formula askew, by turns rewarding and confounding expectations enough to keep viewers off-balance.

This little gem boasts an excellent cast (Gabriel Mann, Candy Clark, Jay Mohr) in fine form under Aussie director Geoffrey Wright (*Romper Stomper,* 1992). It doesn't matter whether you cotton to the film's satiric intent or not: it works well as a thriller and a sly parody. That a honker like *Urban Legends 2* opened theatrically everywhere while *Cherry Falls* was relegated to video and cable limbo is a crime. I don't want to inflate its merits too much, but thriller and horror fans will find *Cherry Falls* well worth a look. *(All the horror movies discussed above are rated 'R' for language, nudity, adult and sexual situations, casual alcohol and drug use, and violence.)*[70]

---

[70] Portions of the above column appeared in *The Chicopee Herald,* February 21-27, 2001, pp. 10, 13., and in *VMag* #39, March 2001, pg. 29; in *Vmag,* the editor chose to add a note ridiculing my *Cherry Falls* review (why publish my review at

February 22:

The indy film phenomenon of *The Blair Witch Project* (1999) divided audiences.[71] The film either worked for you, or it didn't, and those who hated the film were as outspoken as those who reveled in the experience (despite the hard-sell and creative piracy from *The Last Broadcast*,[72] I enjoyed *The Blair Witch Project* on its own terms as a simplistic Lovecraftian 'weird tale' with a nifty stinger in the tail). The inevitable *first* sequel (yes, more are in the works[73]) ***BOOK OF SHADOWS: BLAIR WITCH 2*** (2000) is a tall tale of another kind altogether: it cost millions to make, self-reflexively acknowledges the success of the original film, and eschews the calculated "home-made" hand-held camera work that induced motion-sickness in susceptible *Blair Witch* viewers. Not that the film doesn't leave one dizzy, mind you.

The producers' scheme to tap accomplished documentary filmmaker Joe Berlinger (co-director of the excellent *Brother's Keeper*, 1992, and genuinely terrifying *Paradise Lost: The Child Murders at Robin Hood Hills*,

---

all?), which prompted me to quietly cease contributing reviews to *Vmag*, which ended with that issue in any case.

[71] See *Blur, Vol. 1*, pp. 79-88, 101.

[72] See *Blur, Vol. 1*, pp. 136-138, 176-182.

[73] This proved to be the only theatrically released sequel; one direct-to-video compilation of two sequel featurettes was released in April, 2001 as *The Massacre of the Burkittsville 7: The Blair Witch Legacy*; see *Blur, Vol. 1*, pp. 85-88.

1996)[74] was a good one. Among the resentful residents of tourist-besieged Burkittsville is an angry, opportunistic local (goateed Jeffery Donovan) selling souvenirs online and leading eager tour groups into the supposedly-haunted Black Hills. But this lad with an attitude has a checkered past. After his tour group's late-night bacchanal winds down, they all wake up with hangovers, unable to recall the night before... but they have a sneaking suspicion *something* nasty went down. The ragtag group bundle off to the local yokel's remote warehouse abode as fragmented memories, tell-tale clues, psychic visions, and increasingly malevolent (and seemingly arcane) forces tear at their fragile peace of mind. The body count rises in short order, sending *Book of Shadows* veering into the kind of teen-angst bloodshed its source feature so blithely sidestepped.

This is the antithesis of *The Blair Witch Project*: the production is slick, the narrative convoluted, the climax splintered in too many directions to effectively induce a chill. The film begins well before its tangled web unravels in a multitude of false starts, stops, and conclusions, much like those spiderwebs woven by LSD-spiked arachnids they used to cite during anti-drug lectures. If *Blair Witch* caught its unlikable trio of characters in the

---

[74] Berlinger's involvement also brought the *Blair Witch* legacy full circle, *Blair Witch* having cribbed its premise from *The Last Broadcast* (1998); the co-directors of *Last Broadcast*, Stefan Avalos and Lance Weiler, have always acknowledged their debt to *Paradise Lost*, including its excellent website, which the fictional *Last Broadcast* adapted – pretending its central crime/disappearance was genuine – a conceit *The Blair Witch Project* then 'borrowed' for its internet promotional scheme, which the mass media embraced as being an innovation!

ultimate occult cul-de-sac, *Book of Shadows* loses its brood of equally abrasive saps in a series of blind alleys and dead ends. But don't take my word on *Book of Shadows*, which divided audiences wary of all the ballyhoo: some folks (including friends whose opinions I respect) enjoyed it, some hated it. You know where I sit, but hey, this might be just your cup of tea. I'll check out anything Berlinger directs — *Books of Shadows* is, at least, an interesting failure — but the real-life frissons of *Paradise Lost* will stay with me long after this hokum has faded into shadows. If nothing else, this sequel should put paid to the *Blair Witch* phenomenon, franchise, and backlash, and for that we should be grateful. *(Rated 'R' for nudity, adult and sexual content, violence, gore, casual alcohol and drug use, and lots of confused witchcraft.)*

February 22: **Peter Christian Hall's *DELINQUENT* Portrays Troubles of Teen Years** [75]

It's a cliche, a story we've all seen, read, heard — or lived, in our own way, as teenagers, parents, friends, neighbors — too many times before. A lonely teenager from a broken or abusive home is left to his or her own devices, seeking help, escape, and/or driven to extreme remedies for their insurmountable problems. For a lucky few, help may manifest in time via friends offering help, adults who intercede, or (in rare cases) authorities able and willing to act. For many, many more, self-medication (alcohol, drugs) eases the pain, and they stick it out until they can move on; for others, simply drop-

---

[75] This was *The Brattleboro Reformer* headline for this interview/article.

ping out and running away provides the only available means of escape.

For a few, violence seems the only answer. But through it all, they ache, dream, scheme, and furtively reach for something better — or, simply, an end to the pain.

This, in a nutshell, is the premise of ***DELINQUENT*** (1995/2000), an excellent new independent feature (now on video) that avoids — or invigorates — what have become cliches by confronting the painful realities of teenage loneliness and desperation. Producer / writer / director Peter Christian Hall consciously set out to create a film that eschewed the cliche. *"Most movies about teenagers are terrible, and a lot of them are pretty destructive, like brain-eating candy,"* Peter says. *"Everything works out in the end, through some empty heroic gesture, and no one has to think about anything meaningful. I like stuff that provokes thought and emotion."*

In *Delinquent*, Hall conjures the grim reality and urgent fantasies of his teenage protagonists, Tim (Desmond Devenish) and Tracy (Shawn Batten), with tactile immediacy, weaving the collision of Tim's daydreams against their increasingly dire situation into a haunting tapestry. The final act of this taut drama crackles, plunging towards its seemingly inevitable destination with unexpected, devastating impact. Enlivened by an extraordinary soundtrack by Gang of Four and others, *Delinquent* stands tall among the best new releases on the video shelves.

With his first feature, Peter Hall captures all the longing, frustration, agony and ire of put-upon, aimless youth. He knows the turf all too well; indeed, *Delinquent* is somewhat autobiographical in nature. When asked about the reference to *"an exquisitely painful and mobile adolescence"* in his own biography, Peter admits that *Delinquent* is *"a kind of emotional portrait of my adolescence in a small town in the Hudson Valley,"* embodied in the fictional town of Cold Mills.

In the film, 15-year old Tim is brutalized by his alcoholic policeman father (Jeff Paul) and plagued by memories of having discovered the body of his mother (Ruby Mitchell) after she'd committed suicide; the emotional landscape is close to that of Peter's youth. *"My father was a very tormented, unsuccessful inventor,"* Peter says. *"My mother suffered a lot of mental problems; my sister committed suicide; I was a big underachiever, dismissed from a boarding school."* In the film, the only positive adult attention in Tim's life comes from his English teacher (Marisa Townshend), a detail also drawn from Peter's life: *"I even had a pair of pretty attractive English teachers who helped me a lot in 9th grade by respecting me and privately assigning me lots of great literature -* Catch 22, The Immoralist, Portrait Of The Artist As A Young Man, *etc. I somehow chose to survive it all, and* Delinquent *is my meditation on the emotional price of survival."*

In fact, the reading and writing sparked by those teachers directly fueled *Delinquent*. *"Sherwood Anderson's short-story collection* Winesburg, Ohio *was the first book loaned to me by one of those 9th grade teachers,"* Peter recalls, noting that tome's inspiration (along with films like *If...,* 1968, *Lacombe Lucien,* 1974, *The River's Edge,* 1986, and others). *"Mostly I wrote down everything I cared about for each of those years — 8th grade through 11th — what I read, listened to, watched, my sexual fantasies, ambitions, friends, etc., and I relived as much of it as I could while I took notes on the things that most excited me as issues."*

Peter survived his own difficult adolescence to earn his Master's degree at Columbia University's School of International and Public Affairs and become a successful journalist. Working his way up from journeyman reporting for the *Times Herald-Record* of Middletown, NY to freelance for *Rolling Stone, The Village Voice, Mother Jones*, and other magazines, Peter eventually landing the executive editor position at *Financial World*. His journalism background also informs *Delinquent*. His Upstate New York tenure reporting gave him *"a very good sense of the infinite weirdness of the region, plus a lot of useful stuff like the sloppy rules regarding the hiring of poorly-trained, part-time cops,"* like Tim's father. Still, he has applied some artistic license to his first feature: *"The movie's two lies are that the fictitious Town of Cold Mills would still have a police force, and that it never rains or gets cloudy up there."*

While a journalist, Peter returned to Columbia to study film for two semesters. Dabbling in other media by mounting painting exhibitions and producing multimedia anti-war benefit concerts (featuring Sonic Youth, Ann Magnuson, and others, including Barbara Louise Gogan who contributes the song *"The Perfect Bride"* to *Delinquent*'s soundtrack), Peter also began to write financial/industry videos, music videos, and screenplays. This culminated in *Delinquent*, sans any prior experimentation with short narrative films. *"Perhaps because I was a journalist,"* Peter says, *"it's hard for me to write a short because I come up with too much stuff. Everything becomes feature-length, but I like tight features."* (Peter is currently working on a number of screenplays, including one of which may become his second feature, *Lot's Daughters*. Ever the confrontationalist, Peter notes it's *"about a young American Nazi who somewhat acci-*

dentally nerve gasses a shopping mall. It's my meditation on Tim McVeigh, among other things, and it was — indirectly — Biblically inspired by an Old Testament painting.")[76]

Delinquent 'cost' Peter *"about five years, from the start of writing,"* and was completed for about $300,000. *"I shot it in 1993,"* Peter continues, *"with ten additional shots in 1995. We had three shoots totaling four weeks. Except for two scenes in New Jersey and Brooklyn, everything was shot in Otsego and Chenango counties, about 80 to 115 miles southwest of Albany, New York."* This region was true to Peter's own adolescent landscapes. *"I was raised in the lower Hudson Valley, which is quite suburban now, but my home town was really small at the time, though the high school was a lot bigger. Cold Mills feels a lot like my roots, and we sure wandered around a lot after school looking for trouble in woods and fields."*

The editing process was decidedly unusual. *"I edited the movie twice!,"* Peter exclaims. *"I edited for several months in late 1993 and early '94 and finished the movie in 16 mm in the summer of 1994. That's the version that premiered in Palm Springs and was warmly reviewed in* Variety.*"* Peter subsequently shot additional material, recut the film (trimming six minutes and adding other crucial footage), *"got two more songs from Gang of Four, remixed the sound into Ultra*Stereo, blew the negative up to 35 mm, and reissued it to festivals."*

In fact, Gang of Four contributed more than just their music to the film. *"I had met them while writing*

---

[76] At the time of this writing – August 2008 – *Delinquent* remains Peter Hall's only completed feature.

about them years earlier," Peter says, *"and I sent them the script for comment because John King and Andy Gill are both very literate film fanatics. They critiqued the script and volunteered to write the score, so I'd send them scenes on videotape and they'd whip things up. Andy in particular really understood what I was up to, and I think he relished being told to crank up his guitar, whereas filmmakers had always asked him to sweeten his sound. Much of the music wound up on their CD, 'Shrinkwrapped,' which I like a lot."*

Despite four years of festival playdates, rave reviews from top-drawer newspapers and magazines, and eventual theatrical distribution in over a dozen states, *Delinquent* still had a difficult time securing a video venue. *"It's a hideous thought that the* LA Times *could say your movie makes them believe 'in the possibility of truly independent American cinema' and you reap nothing from it but bragging rights, but that's what happened,"* Peter sighs.

Thankfully, *Delinquent* is now on video. Though the video box art depends upon the most obvious caricaturization of the film's title — the angry, violent j.d. pointing a gun at the viewer — the film itself plays against the sensational archetype. Somewhat uncomfortable with the present marketing (though he did ultimately approve it), Peter notes, *"I didn't call it* THE Delinquent *because I really think the adults in the movie are all delinquent, except for the schoolteacher."*

The structure of the film — playing out Tim's fantasies in 'real time,' as if they were actual events, before bringing the viewer back to reality after each dream or fantasy plays itself out — is quite unique. This unusual approach to the story evolved organically, even as Peter shot and edited his feature. *"The first dream sequence was always there,"* he explains. *"I really wanted to get a distinctive take on human consciousness, especially the glorious confusion that occurs when you wake up under duress, as the real world forces new information into your dream state till it dissolves. I expanded all this while we were shooting, so I added the school-teacher fantasy and made the ending both dreamier and more disturbing. I definitely like to jump back and forth between mental states, with as few visual cues as I can get away with. That's reality, as far as I'm concerned."*

Caught in this waking dream state, Tim is literally 'delinquent' (thus, another play on the title): unable, or afraid, to act on his every impulse. *"I think he means well enough, but he's been driven to a kind of hopeless passivity,"* Peter says, speaking from his own experiences. *"I think kids are inclined to be passive until they feel a kind of group spirit afoot, a buzz. Tim's a loner, and he has no blueprint for how things can work well. He's only seen catastrophe in his recent life, which obviously has undermined whatever else he saw before his father lost his job and house, and his mother took her life."*

Thankfully, the lead performances by Desmond Devenish and Shawn Batten enfuse Tim and Tracy with engaging life. Unlike typical Hollywood movie teenagers played by pros in their twenties, Desmond was the real thing. *"Desmond was just finishing high school,"* Peter recalls. *"Desmond was a surprise, because I kept thinking I'd ultimately pick someone else, but his work was always fascinating enough that I'd have to invite him back to contend again. Particularly when I reviewed his auditions on video, it was clear that the camera understood him perfectly, captured little moves you could hardly see in the live performance."* Shawn was not a teenager, having just earned her B.A. prior to filming: *"I chose Shawn because she was very professional and very determined; most potential Tracys were reading their lines like victims, whereas Shawn's physical and mental self-confidence would make it that much more powerful if her character ran out of steam."*

In the wake of various recent tragedies involving young men and guns (Columbine the most prominent among them), *Delinquent* plucks a particularly vital collective nerve — and prompts thoughts and conclusions far different than those offered by most pundits and media fare. As both a filmmaker and journalist, Peter has his own strong views on our collective national response, or lack of same, to such tragedies. *"I was trying to tell the truth in* Delinquent,*"* he says, *"not to tell people what to think, but to ask questions that wouldn't dissolve with the credits. Since it was made years before Columbine, that tells me that there are indefinable truths swimming in the movie. As I look at the things I choose to write about, I'm always struck that I'm obsessed with why good people do terrible things. But just as no one really solves anything in* Delinquent*, except in Tim's peculiarly very costly fashion, I don't think this country solved anything after Columbine."*

"It's probably more trying than ever to be a weird, unpopular kid in high school, because now people say you're going to murder them," Peter concludes. *"We used to joke about our 'machine gun list' in college, and tell our friends how they rated on a given day; we just didn't have any real interest in the guns themselves. I think most such events get served up as titillating 'news' entertainment, and then are forgotten until someone crassly exploits them on camera, complete with a contrived 'happy' ending. I hope I will always sympathize*

with young people who are learning how to function in what I consider to be a cruel world. And I'm glad I wasn't raised now, because I would have had insane problems for a lot of things that simply were not significant, and which only I can remember. I guess I think people should listen to one another; one of things I like best in Delinquent *is that everyone yells at Tim for not listening, but no one hears anything he's trying to tell them."*

Thankfully, Peter Christian Hall listens, remembers, and speaks his mind.

His is a fresh voice and vision, and *Delinquent* is definitely a 'must see' film.[77]

March 1:

Veteran actress Sally Fields must have thought she was onto something while helming Minnie Driver through the agonizing throes of ***BEAUTIFUL*** (2000), but she was sadly mistaken. This miserably unfunny comedy traces the rise and fall of American Miss Junior Miss contestant Ramona (Driver), who will do anything — *anything* — to win the title. Unfortunately, we've all been here before Sally or Minnie, who have nothing new to bring to the podium. Two films trod the same ground with far better results — Michael Ritchie's sly gem *Smile* (1975), and last year's nastier, bawdier *Drop Dead Gorgeous* [78] — either of which delivers a richer evening's entertainment than this turgid embarrassment. Minnie Driver fans should run for the hills, and Sally

---

[77] Peter's website is still accessible at the time of this writing: http://www.metal-tiger.com/delinquent
[78] See *Blur, Vol. 1*, pg. 146.

Field followers should hang their heads; you can't polish a cowpie. *(Rated "PG-13" for harsh language, mild slapstick, and sexual innuendoes.)*

BEDAZZLED (2000) is the latest from writer/director Harold Ramis, who emerged from the cutting-edge of '70s comedy (*National Lampoon*, etc.), but remains best known for his role as Egon from *Ghostbusters* (1984). Egon's deadpan know-it-all manner informs Ramis' better filmmaking efforts (from the ragged but funny *Caddyshack*, 1980; *National Lampoon's Vacation*, 1983; *Groundhog Day*, 1993; *Stuart Saves His Family*, 1994), but one can't help but think that Egon would dismiss Ramis' increasingly mainstream recent efforts (*Multiplicity*, 1996; *Analyze This*, 1998) with a well-deserved sneer. Further evidence of Ramis' decline plagues this 2000 remake of Stanley Donen's 1967 British original.

As in Donen's swinging London version, a contemporary spin on the old Faustian deal-with-the-devil motif invites disaster as wishes for a better life (i.e., love, wealth, sensitivity, happiness) are perverted into unexpected avenues and incarnations. In place of 1967's Peter Cook, Dudley Moore, and Racquel Welch, Ramis gives us Brendan Fraser as yet another hapless nitwit (grow a brain or get a better agent, Brendan!) wrapped around the finger of devil Elizabeth Hurley, who twists Fraser's seven wishes into ruin. Tisn't funny, coming across as a one-dimensional retread of both the '67 *Bedazzled* (which was uneven, but conjured its own magic) and Ramis' brilliant *Groundhog Day*. Maybe the devil (or the dollars) made him do it. *(Rated "PG-13" for strong language, adult and sexual situations, casual alcohol and drug use/abuse, some violence.)*

GET CARTER is the latest Sylvester Stallone vehicle, and also evidence of a star in decline. In search of his brother's killer, Jack Carter (Stallone) stalks with one-note malevolence through director Stephen Kay's Seattle-based remake of the 1971 Brit mini-classic *Get Carter*. Michael Caine was the star of the original (both derived from Ted Lewis' 1970 novel *Jack's Return Home*), and he pops up here as one of the shady characters Stallone muscles for information, lending some sorely-needed credentials to this decidedly lackluster affair. Director Kay dresses the mayhem up with contemporary reference points, fractured editing techniques, and flashy cinematography, much as director Steven Soderbergh (*Sex, Lies and Videotape*, 1989, *Erin Brockovich, Traffic*, both 2000, etc.) gussied up his recent *Get Carter* revamp *The Limey* (2000)[79] with disorienting flashbacks and flashforwards. However, Soderbergh did so with purpose as well as style; Kay indulges such flourishes as if to make up for inherent weaknesses.

He should have trusted his source material and peeled his pretensions to raw sinew and bone. The original *Get Carter* (which recently earned a position in the UK film zine *Empire* top-crime films lineup, and is highly recommended) stands tall for its seedy, caustic drive, emulating the stoic obsessiveness of Jack Carter himself, letting nobody and nothing stand in his way whatever the outcome. This remake is a pale shadow at best. Give Stallone credit for gravitating to worthy source material; too bad he and his collaborators fudge it so badly. Before you belittle Sly too much, note that Mel Gibson recently stumbled in a similar manner (and in the

---

[79] See *Blur, Vol. 1*, pp. 241-243.

same genre) by remaking John Boorman's seminal 1967 *Point Blank* (adapted from Richard Stark's novel *The Hunter*, 1963) as the mean-but-merely-okay *Payback* (1998). Someone should lean on these stooges. Get Carter, indeed. *(Rated "R" for strong language, violence, gunplay, adult and sexual situations, alcohol and drug abuse.)*

WHEN PIGS FLY (1993), however, is an original. Given all the remakes — ghosts of movies past — choking the new release wall, it's comforting to find something fresh stretching out in the boneyard. Here's a genuine ghost story blossoming amid a welcome resurrection of the genre (*The Sixth Sense, A Stir of Echoes*), though this urban parable actually predated the late 1990s revival with an affectionate view of spectral visitors and their influence on the mortals in their thrall. Sara Driver and Ray Dobbins' *When Pigs Fly* has just been re-released to video, as bracing and beguiling as can be, dancing with comical serenity toward its satisfying climactic eruption of supernatural ire and sweet release.

When an outgoing New York stripper (Maggie O'Neill) tries to coax her landlord, an agoraphobic jazz pianist (Alfred Molina of *Boogie Nights*, 1997, *Chocolat,* 2000, etc.), out of his insular squalor with the gift of an antique chair lifted from a bar's storeroom, she has no idea that the chair is haunted... or that her gift will ultimately have the desired effect in spades. The performers — including Marianne Faithful and youngster Rachael Bella as the ghosts Lilly and Ruthie, who died a century apart on the same seat — are in top form, and the film's portrait of mingled lives and afterlives is charming and compelling throughout.

Fans of indy director Jim Jarmusch (*Stranger Than Paradise,* 1982, *Mystery Train,* 1989, *Dead Man,* 1995, *Ghost Dog: The Way of the Samurai,* 1999, etc.), take note: Jarmusch co-executive-produced this gem. Though he insisted his role not be inflated for publicity purposes, *When Pigs Fly* does share Jarmusch's deadpan wit, hangdog pacing, and affection for urban misfits seeking redemption. Jarmusch was justified in his stance, though, as director Sara Driver (who co-scripted with Ray Dobbins) nurtures a distinctive cinematic voice and vision with its own seductive tenor and tone. Celebrated cinematographer Robby Müller (*The American Friend/Der Amerikanische Freund,* 1977, *Repo Man* and *Paris, Texas,* both 1984, *Breaking the Waves,* 1996, a clutch of Jarmusch's films, a lots more) and the wistful score by Joe Strummer (of The Clash) put the icing on the cake. Give this gem a shot; it's much, much better than most of this month's 'major' releases. Recommended! *(Unrated, but this would most probably earn a "PG-13" for its language and casual alcohol abuse.)*

March 8:
The 10th Women's Film Festival: Silent classics, Australian Ghosts

The 10th Anniversary Women's Film Festival[80] continues with tonight's debut double features. Both double-bills offer documentaries about the creators of

---

[80] This is one of Brattleboro, VT's ongoing annual cinema events worth celebrating, one I supported whenever I could via this column; see *Blur, Vol. 1*, pp. 229-234. Note that I've edited the venue and time listings from this reprint.

their companion feature films, eloquently book-ending almost a century of dynamic women's cinema.

Bridget Terry and Cari Beauchamp's ***WITHOUT LYING DOWN: FRANCES MARION AND THE POWERFUL WOMEN OF EARLY HOLLYWOOD*** (2000) accompanies ***THE POOR LITTLE RICH GIRL*** (1917), Frances Marion's first collaborative effort with 'America's Sweetheart' Mary Pickford, one of the silent era's first and most beloved stars.

Frances Marion was among Hollywood's most prolific and highest-paid screenwriters of the silent era. Before studio patriarchs prompted Marion to channel her creative energies elsewhere in the 1930s, she scripted over 200 feature films, winning two Academy Awards and founding genres that have remained staples. Born Frances Owens, she was an accomplished author, artist, and model as a youth, moving to Los Angeles during cinema's formative years. In 1914, popular screen comedienne Marie Dressler urged Frances to engage with the Hollywood scene. Changing her name to Frances Marion, she worked as an actress, stunt woman, set mover, and film editor until she met rising star Mary Pickford. They became lifelong friends. Pickford's appreciation for Frances' talents prompted her to invite Frances to script *The Poor Little Rich Girl*, against the wishes of powerful director Cecil B. DeMille; DeMille was soon replaced by French director Maurice Tourneur.

The Poor Little Rich Girl (based on the 1913 Broadway play by Eleanor Gates) is still a charmer. 24-year-old Pickford gives a surprisingly credible performance as 11-year-old Gwendolyn, the titular girl raised amid metropolitan wealth but denied fundamental parental love or childhood companions. Pickford, Marion, and Tourneur took creative chances which studio head Alfred Zucker despised (almost derailing the film's release), but audiences loved. We see Gwen's mental pictures of adult phrases that bewilder her (Wall Street 'bears,' 'a snake in the grass,' servants referred to as 'two-faced' and 'big-eared,' etc.); the disorienting effects of a servant's narcotic overdose of Gwen prompts delirium dreams and a final act that anticipates the framing structure of MGM's 1939 classic *The Wizard of Oz*. The archetypal wellspring for countless *"poor little rich kids"* like *Richie Rich*, this film remains a delight.

The Poor Little Rich Girl was an enormous international success, initiating a fertile collaborative period for Marion and Pickford that ended with *The Love Light* (1920), which Marion scripted and directed. Thereafter, Marion scripted features for other stars, including westerns for her husband Fred Thomson and two Lillian Gish classics, *The Scarlet Letter* (1926) and *The Wind* (1928). Marion adapted readily to the coming of sound, co-founding the Screen Writers' Guild and resurrecting the dormant career of her dear friend Marie Dressler on the way.

Without Lying Down is narrated by Uma Thurman and features Kathy Bates reading from Marion's letters and memoirs. This excellent overview of Marion's remarkable life and career harbors one distinct echo of the patriarchal mogul system that brought Marion's (and Mary Pickford's) reign to an end: the film was executive produced for Turner Movie Classics by none other than Hugh Hefner. Marion, no doubt, would have winced at the irony.

Australian photographer/writer/director Tracey Moffat seizes the spotlight with the double-bill of Jane

Cole's documentary *UP IN THE SKY: TRACEY MOFFAT IN NEW YORK* (1999) and Moffat's feature directorial debut, *BEDEVIL* (2000).

Jane Cole's *Up in the Sky* chronicles Moffat's rise in the international photography scene, culminating in her prestigious NYC exhibition at the Dia Center for the Arts (1997-98). En route, Cole details Moffat's key photographic works, *"Backyard Series"* (1974), *"Something More"* (1989), *"Scarred for Life"* (1995), and the titular series *"Up in the Sky"* (1997). Amusing as it is to see Moffat hobnob with art dealers, curators, and patrons of the fickle metropolitan art market, Moffat's distinctive voice and vision resonates apart from such elitist trappings.

Facing the camera, Moffat says, *"Life's a battle — don't you think?,"* summarizing the ire and art, heart and heartbreak that drives her work. Moffat, a part-aboriginal women raised in an adoptive white household, seems eternally drawn to intimate domestic hells. The painful tableaus of her *"Scarred Life"* series and the narrative impetus of her *"Up in the Sky"* photographs fuels her early filmwork. Moffat's own documentary *Solid Women* (1989) and later *Nice Colored Girls* aren't cited, but Cole does excerpt Moffat's video *Heaven* and the harrowing *Night Cries: A Rural Tragedy* (1990), which Moffat describes as a semi-autobiographical piece *"about loving and hating your mother."* In a claustrophobic Outback homestead, a black middle-aged daughter cares for her elderly, dying white mother; the pain is palpable in the static tableaus, stylized soundtrack, and oversaturated colors.

Spirits are high in more ways than one in Moffat's *BeDevil* (that's the onscreen title; completed in 1994), the first Australian feature by an Aborigine and a mischievous meditation on rural legends the artist grew up with. As in *Night Cries*, Moffat orchestrates a cunning fusion of exterior locations and stylized studio environments, creating an uneasy tension between the blazing Outback landscape of her native country and the fabricated 'interior dreamscapes' of her imagination. *BeDevil* is, essentially, an omnibus film, offering a trio of enigmatic reveries: *"Mr Chuck"* is a swamp spirit (Benjamin Collard) awakened when an aboriginal boy (Ben Kennedy) vandalizes a cinema built over the marsh. Moffat appears in the playful *"Choo Choo Choo Choo,"* set in a home along the tracks plagued by lights in the sky, unnerving stick dolls, a spectral blind girl, and ghost trains. *"Lovin' the Spin I'm In"* finds the teenage son (Riccardo Natoli) of a landlord (Lex Marinos) drawn to the plight of the tenants his father plans to evict, including an old woman (Pinua Ghee) still mourning a long-dead son and lover who haunt the warehouse below.

Moffat eschews conventional linear narratives to conjure fragmented glimpses of lives (and afterlives) literally on the edge: of a swamp, the tracks, the sea. Moffat makes exquisite use of Carl Vine's engaging score, Stephen Curtis' sets, and Geoff Burton's ravishing cinematography. From the opening images as emerald rivulets of water shimmer amid rippled beach sand, drifting into the browned vegetation and bubbling, brackish tarn of a swamp, Moffat's elemental imagery has a primal allure. With its eerie ambience and wry humor, *BeDevil* indeed bewitches.

March 8:

For all our supposed shared loathing of 1950s McCarthyism, we've sure endured our share of witch hunts of late. Will we never learn? In light of the ongoing investigations our recently departed ex-prez continues to attract, the issues raked over the coals in ***THE CONTENDER*** (2000) are as timely as they were when this fine political drama hit theaters last year. But the film has much more going for it than mere topicality. *The Contender* is an entertaining slice of drama boasting a stellar cast at the top of their game, a solid script spiced with venom and wit, and — most unexpected of all — a clarity of perception and intent. Multi-million dollar studio 'product' isn't supposed to be this savvy, smart, or concerned about our political process.

The Presidency of Democrat Jackson Evans (Jeff Bridges, a looooong way from "The Dude" of *The Big Lebowski*, 1998) is challenged by the death of the Vice President and the subsequent scramble for a replacement. The bid of *"the candidate most likely"* (William Peterson of *To Live and Die in L.A.*, 1985, *Manhunter*, 1986, *The Skulls*, 2000, etc.) is tragically compromised by his failed attempt to rescue a drowning woman whose car plunged from a bridge. But Evans' embittered Republican political rival Congressman Shelly Runyon (Gary Oldman of *Sid and Nancy*, 1986, *The Professional*, 1994, *Hannibal*, 2001, etc., excellent in another toxic role) is sharpening his knives to cut down the President's pick, Senator Laine Hanson (Joan Allen, who's previous brush with the Presidency as First Lady spiced Oliver Stone's *Nixon*, 1995). Aided by ambitious freshman Representative Reginald Webster (Christian Slater) and the spotlight of televised hearings, Runyon mounts an intimidating attack on Senator Hanson's past *"indiscretions,"* fomenting a personalized sexual scandal that may or may not be rooted in truth.

The Contender is that rare item: a Hollywood production which brings the courage of its convictions to its political content, and (rarer still) does so in a thinly-fictionalized Washington D.C. that acknowledges the often ruthless partisan savagery between Republicans and Democrats. Contemporary sexual and gender politics are ruthlessly probed, justifying the role-reversal necessary to the plot (supplanting President Clinton's infamous sexual debacle with the brutal scrutiny of Senator Hanson's private life). More fundamentally, the script questions the schism between personal and public life, and whether belief in inherent human truth, dignity, decency, and honor can possibly withstand the corruptive forces drawn by their very nature to such bases of power.

Writer/director Rod Lurie (*Deterrence*, 1999) cannily dissects the Machiavellian schemes, 'Good Ol' Boy' networking, and harrowing closed-door bloodbaths that culminate in the broadcast and print arenas where cynical bids to manipulate public perception are played out like hands of blackjack. The echoes of history are transparent — the Ted Kennedy Chappaquiddick scandal, Bill & Monica, Kenneth Starr — but Lurie deftly incorporates *and* undercuts the associative baggage these real-life events bring to his imaginary 'what if' scenario. Though the final act succumbs somewhat to Lurie's own brand of piety (the writer can't resist soap boxing in the end), he flaunts his trump card only after the riveting final hand has been properly played. (Much as I admire the sentiments of Evans' final speech, I know I'll never in my lifetime hear a president embrace, much less voice, such decency.)

The DVD is particularly noteworthy. Aside from the format's inherent superior transfer of audio and visual elements, *The Contender* DVD also showcases a dozen scenes cut from the final version that are sorely missed. The film plays well without them, with Lurie's commentary track noting the valid reasons for the trims, but all the scenes do add considerable depth to the story and characters. The feature can also be viewed with an engaging commentary track from writer/director Lurie and star Joan Allen, which is also recommended.

You don't have to subscribe to any particular political party to enjoy *The Contender*, nor is it a prerequisite that you harbor a healthy disgust for the vicious hypocrisy of the Ken Starr era of sexual interrogation (I, for one, shudder whenever I hear government authorities castigate the media in the wake of the Starr report; who do they think they're fooling any longer?). But you do need to keep your eyes, ears, and heart open — and don't look away from Joan Allen for a heartbeat, as she delivers one of the year's best performances. Highly recommended! *(Rated "R" for very strong language, sometimes vivid sexual situations and innuendo, and truly adult drama.)*

March 15:

The autobiographical ***ALMOST FAMOUS*** (2000) reminds us that writer/director Cameron Crowe was indeed a child prodigy. He was writing for *Cream* and *Rolling Stone* before his sixteenth birthday. His sociological/autobiographical take on covertly returning to high school (in his twenties, Crowe still looked young enough to pass for a teenager) was an instant best-seller, and made the jump from page to screen as *Fast Times at Ridgemont High* (1982), earning Crowe his first screenplay credit. *Fast Times* remains the smartest, most insightful of all '80s teen flicks, and Crowe established himself as one of his generation's clearest voices. Building on that accomplishment, Crowe scripted *The Wild Life* (1984) and thereafter wrote *and* directed *Say Anything* (1989), *Singles* (1992), and scored a breakthrough hit with *Jerry Maguire* (1996). Like I said, the lad's a prodigy. After *Jerry Maguire*, Crowe could have had anything. Thankfully, he rolled his newfound *"Show me the money!"* cache into *Almost Famous* (2000), a fresh, funny, and moving portrait of Crowe's coming-of-age on the road with a touring '70s rock'n'roll band.

Crowe's surrogate screen self is William Miller (Patrick Fugit), a misfit 15-year old senior with a flair for writing and deep love of rock music. Cutting his teeth with a gig for *Cream* magazine under the tutelage of editor and legendary rock critic Lester Bangs (Philip Seymour Hoffman), Will lands an assignment for *Rolling Stone* covering a local concert featuring the up-and-coming band Stillwater. Beneath the wing of 'not-a-groupie' band sweetheart Penny Lane (Kate Hudson), Will gets his foot in the door backstage and makes contact with Stillwater's lead guitarist Russell Hammond (Billy Crudup), who invites the boy wonder to their next tour stop and promises an interview. With the reluctant permission of his mother (Frances McDormand) and long-distance, late-night phone guidance of mentor Bangs, Will boards the bus, setting this marvelous film's narrative wheels in motion.

The tour, of course, becomes Will's rite of passage into adulthood in more ways than one, and the boy inadvertently becomes the catalyst for Penny's, Russell's, and the band's painful coming of age. Capturing the heady stew of drugs, sex, and rock'n'roll (which by turns enhances and deadens the sensory overload of the tour experience), Crowe fashions a winning recreation of the era and events he came of age within, maintaining a compassionate focus on his characters and their volatile chemistry. We are lucky enough to share Will's bracing ride into the whitewater of the second-string rock scene, first love (he of course falls for Penny), and sexual initiation, all the while under the gun of a high-pressure deadline, imminent fame (for the band as well as himself), and the tug of the umbilical cord home.

Dear to Crowe's and the film's heart is Penny Lane, brought to stunning life by Kate Hudson's beguiling performance (which deservedly won her a Golden Globe and should win her the Oscar for Best Supporting Actress). Early in the film, Penny confides in Will that Russell is her most important *"project,"* thus elevating herself (in her own mind, at least) beyond lowly groupie status to engage with the creative growth of her beloved Russell. As played by Hudson, Penny is a worldly pixie who revels in the roles of nurturer, muse, and lover. She prides herself as an anchor amid the lunatic rootlessness of the road, though the arrested adolescents she lavishes her attention upon seem incapable of rewarding her devotions in kind (Will, of course, aches to prove himself worthy — but alas, heartbreak awaits). Evoking Pamela Des Barres' portrait of the lifestyle in her book *I'm With the Band: Confessions of a Groupie* (1987), Crowe lovingly styles a valentine to the Penny Lanes of the world without indulging the fantasies the archetype arouses, and Hudson breathes fragile life into the role with often breathtaking skill.

Like the band itself, *Almost Famous* skates a reckless, razor-thin tightrope, threatening to break apart any second with a single misstep or inappropriate word. Amid the fickle crowds, ego-battles, head-games and sexual musical-chairs, Crowe and his mop-top surrogate Will keep their wits about them by keeping their eyes wide open. Among the film's grace notes is a quiet reconciliation aboard the tour bus, as the band's imminent disintegration is averted by a shared moment with a lovely tune (Elton John's *"Tiny Dancer"*) that rekindles the bonds between all on board. Crowe captures the fragile emotional shift with perfect pitch, sparking our own memories of people, places, and music dear to a generation, while inviting us to sing along, too (and you will). This is one of the season's best films, and you owe yourself the experience. *(Rated 'R' for strong language, casual alcohol and drug use and abuse, nudity, adult and sexual situations.)*

Like *Almost Famous*, **WONDER BOYS** (2000) is a coming of age tale; the rites-of-passage herein involves a fifty-year-old English Professor, but it's a coming of age tale nonetheless. Sadly, unlike *Almost Famous*, this canny adaptation of Michael Chabon's novel *Wonder Boys* failed to click at the box-office, despite a tentative theatrical re-release timed to inflate Academy Award attention. One can only hope home video paves the way to the audience the film deserves.

A thumbnail description of the story sounds like bleak going — but it isn't. *Wonder Boys* details the inexorable spiralling fortunes of one-hit novelist and college professor Grady Tripp (Michael Douglas) during a fateful day that culminates in a disastrous literary conference. Whoa, don't start bumming; the film, like the book, maintains a wry, at times hilarious perspective on Tripp's cumulative degradation as his personal and professional mid-life crisis brings his life down around his ears in mere hours. Still struggling with a monstrous, unfinished *"second novel"* (which has swelled from 300 to over 2500 pages), Tripp lives down to his name by stumbling over the tangled threads and affections he has strung across his path. The man is literally his own worst enemy, seemingly programmed for self-destruct and determined to see through the sequential arming of the ticking time bombs he has (unconsciously) set for himself. Amid the shambles of each detonation, Tripp's marriage collapses as his ongoing affair with the Dean's wife (Frances McDormand) unravels with the revelation of her pregnancy. His desperate agent (Robert Downey, Jr.) shows up with a transvestite date in tow, begging for a peek at Tripp's unfinished manuscript before turning his bisexual affections toward one of Tripp's most depressed but gifted students (Toby Maguire), an enigmatic youth who likewise dogs Tripp throughout the evening. This emotional maelstrom soon finds Tripp courting disaster with his lover's dead canine in his car trunk and eluding the police. As the complications grow, we can see that Tripp — an intelligent and worldly fellow, though hardly sober — could, at almost any juncture, defuse the escalating disaster. Instead, Tripp embraces every fresh twist of the blade, proceeding as if he's helpless to avert the inevitable, wondering only how soon it will come, and how much it will hurt.

Steve Klove's witty screenplay inspires a sterling cast to deliver in spades, headed by Michael Douglas in one of the finest roles of his career. Douglas sinks his teeth into the role of Grady for all he's worth, redeeming a decade of floundering in lead roles defined by lounge lizards, smarmy predators, and weak-chinned heels. Director Curtis Hanson helms with surprising dexterity and assurance, marking an engaging maturation that his lead character here aches to achieve. Once a cineaste and the founder/editor of *Cinema* magazine, Hanson assumed the director's chair with the sordid beach-killer case history *The Arousers* (aka *Sweet Kill*) way back in 1970. After dabbling with juvenilia and made-for-TV fare, Hanson engaged with his apparent genre of choice with the thriller *The Bedroom Window* (1987) and never looked back (*Bad Influence*, 1990; *The Hand That Rocks the Cradle*, 1992; *The River Wild*, 1994). Hanson's breakthrough adaptation of James Ellroy's *L.A. Confidential* (1997) was his first real masterpiece, and it's invigorating to see Hanson build on that accomplishment so quickly. As in *L.A. Confidential*, Hanson coaxes a remarkable ensemble chemistry from a top-drawer cast.

By the way, Frances McDormand fans rejoice: you have *two* excellent showcases for her talents at your fingertips during the same week, in two of the year's best films. Lightening, it seems, can strike twice. *(Rated 'R' for casual alcohol and drug use and abuse, strong language, nudity, adult and sexual situations, and some violence.)*

March 22:

Romantic comedies are a dime a dozen as far as I'm concerned, but **NICE GUYS SLEEP ALONE** (2000) has a breezy tone, genuinely likable cast of characters, and engaging style and pace that I found refreshing. Based on the novel by Bruce Feirstein, writer/producer/director Stu Pollard mounts a lively snapshot of the highs and lows of the contemporary 'thirties' dating scene with a dose of home-grown common sense lacking from similar Hollywood fare.

The film lovingly chronicles the wary gravitational pull between single high school teacher Carter Wagner

(Sean O'Bryan) and transplanted New York veterinarian Maggie (Sybil Temchen), who finds herself put off by the 'Southern Gentlemen' courtship rituals she encounters. While Carter advises his own students to *"not play games with other people's hearts,"* both characters initially succumb to the *"sage advice"* and match-making efforts of their respective best friends, Pat (Blake Steury) and Kate (Brenda James) — and thereby hangs the tale.

The engaging cast, cunning banter, crisp cinematography, and lovely Louiseville, Kentucky settings are nicely orchestrated by Pollard into a fine, funny, and ultimately moving indie gem. Sean O'Bryan (who comes across like Pollard's surrogate sibling in the extras added to both the VHS and DVD presentations) and Sybil Temchen won my heart as they struggled with their own.

Welcome turns by veteran character actor William Sanderson (*Raggedy Man*, 1981, *Blade Runner*, 1982, *Newhart*, 1982-90, etc.) as a kindly horse ranch stallion manager and Michael Green's 'pre-relationship' attorney Slick Willie are the icing on the cake (note that we've got free copies of Slick Willie's 'pre-relationship' contract waiting for you at the store; you never know, they just might come in handy![81]). Pollard's deft handling of a budding romance between two of Carter's students (Jeff Roth and Maggie Lawson) adds a surprisingly delicate grace note the to finale, though it's the hilarious class trip to a nearby horse ranch that literally climaxes in a vivid demonstration (tastefully handled) of horse breeding that will stick in your memory.

---

[81] Copies of the 'pre-relationship' faux-legal documents were a promotional giveaway item we carried at First Run Video, free with every rental of the film.

This is a fine romantic comedy and evening's entertainment, further evidence of the health of the indie film scene. Both the VHS and DVD sport a lively clutch of extras, including a featurette on the making of the film, deleted scenes, outtakes, and trailers. Recommended! *(Unrated, but most likely 'PG-13' status or a very soft 'R' for some adult and sexual situations, language, and offscreen horse coupling.)*[82]

March 29:

CHARLIE'S ANGELS (2000) is the latest big-screen adaptation of a brain-dead TV series (1976-81) has become an unlikely, playful vehicle for turn of the Millennium "grrrrrrrl" power thanks to Drew Barrymore, who produced and costars as one of the titular (no pun intended) 'Angels.' My initial, immediate resolve to never see this no-brainer when it dominated theaters last summer eroded as more and more women who should know better talked about what a good time they had with it.

How and why Barrymore and her costars (fellow Angels Lucy Liu and Cameron Diaz) embraced a vapid 1970s antique renowned for its insipid sexist content (or lack thereof) as a viable proto-feminist polemic will fuel many a thesis, but the simple fact is *Charlie's Angels* is dumb fun (I almost said *"surprisingly dumb fun,"* but

---

[82] Note: Due to eleventh hour space considerations, The Reformer bumped my review of *The Wonder Boys* from March 15 and incorporated it into the March 22 column, hence the brevity of this column.

it's no surprise that this is a dumb movie — just that it *is* indeed fun).

Barrymore wisely surrounds herself with top-drawer talent and celebrities, which is also in tune with the original series' guest stars, glam, and glitter. Bill Murray is Bosley, stumbling through the inane excuse for a plot as the put-upon go-between betwixt the invisible billionaire Charlie and the sassy Angels, Dylan (Barrymore), Natalie (Diaz), and Alex (Liu); Tim Curry and Crispin Glover lend their fringe countercultural credentials (Curry of *Rocky Horror Picture Show*, 1975, Glover of 1986's *River's Edge* infamy) as the nominal Bondian villains; cameos from the likes of Tom Green (offering post-election humor as, ahem, *"The Chad"*) further sweeten the pot.

But it's the Angels who carry the day. Barrymore, Diaz, and Liu's obvious delight in their roles and the gravity-defying post-Matrix martial arts action that keeps them on top of the bad guys is infectious. They get to indulge all manner of fantasies: show-stopping dance numbers, bondage, domination, rescuing Bosley time and time again, wall-to-wall kicking of collective bad-guy butt. *Charlie's Angels* is utterly and unapologetically vapid, shallow, mindless, and silly. I fought as hard as I could, but damn it, I had a good time. *(Rated 'PG-13' for tame sexual innuendos, violence, sexual situations, and partial nudity.)*

Any and all video viewers frustrated with the minimum-wage work scene (and attendant after-hours antics) will find plenty to amuse them in the often hilarious indy gem ***WAITING: THE MOVIE*** (2000). Writer/director Patrick Hasson's rude, raucous comedy is narrated by put-upon twenty-something college grad Sean McNutt

(Will Keenan of *Tromeo and Juliet*, 1996, and *Terror Firmer*, 1999), whose father has given him just thirty days to get out of the old homestead and find his own apartment. Of course, Sean's latest dead-end job — waiting tables at Broccoletti's, a South Philadelphia Italian bistro — barely pays enough to make such a move possible. By his own admission, life is a clogged toilet for loser McNutt, hounded by creditors and aching to patch things up with his ex-girlfriend Andrea (Kerri Kenney) despite her ongoing fling with a lout who delights in tormenting Sean at every turn.

The ribald, often scatological, humor is perfectly in tune with Sean's spiraling fortunes, which constantly finds him struggling to maintain some shred of dignity under increasingly dire circumstances. The bulk of *Waiting* is set in Broccoletti's, where Sean and his fellow underpaid co-workers fume at the customers, each other, and chomp at the bit to squeeze all they can out of their inebriated midnight-to-dawn search for a good time. The sex-capades are lively fun, peppered with a free-for-all crosscutting between couplings that's abruptly interrupted by a misplaced corkscrew, and the opportunistic revenge exacted by one of Sean's dominatrix ex-girlfriends. The inevitable confrontations with unruly customers (including porn star Ron Jeremy, who also cameoed in *Orgazmo*, 1997, and the First Rites feature *Art House*, 1998) are amusing, too; proprietor Nick Broccoletti's protracted reverie about losing his virginity, related at great length to put an unruly woman seeking a free meal in her place, is particularly memorable.

Producer John Stefanic and writer/director Hasson mount an affectionate, infectious insider's peek at the restaurant work scene sure to delight and disgust viewers (and prompt more than a few concerns about one's next dining experience). The entire ensemble cast is in fine form, but scruffy lead player Will Keenan is particularly appealing throughout (winning a Best Actor Award for his efforts from the Williamsburg Brooklyn Film Festival). Whether he's insulting Andrea's father (a cameo played by Troma honcho Lloyd Kaufman), spurning the advances of the diapered middle-aged *"Baby Poo Poo"* in a fringe club, or spraying shaving cream into his mouth to clear his alcohol-tainted breath before the cops pull him over, Keenan is a spry and immensely likable screen presence who effortlessly carries the film.

Waiting targets the filmmakers' immediate peer group — college students, twenty-something wage slaves, and young adults who will identify completely with Sean and his compadres — but there's plenty here to amuse one and all here. I quite liked this scrappy comedy; Recommended! *(Unrated, but would most likely earn an 'R' for its strong language, nudity, adult and sexual situations, scatalogical gags, and casual alcohol and drug use.)*

March 29: Filmmaker Stu Pollard explains why NICE GUYS SLEEP ALONE

Like his first feature film ***NICE GUYS SLEEP ALONE*** (2000), producer/writer/director Stu Pollard has an easy grace and sense of style that's irresistible. Working from the novel by Bruce Feirstein, Pollard's debut feature (now on video and DVD) offers an engaging glimpse at the contemporary 'thirties' dating scene. True to the spirit of the classic romantic comedies of decades past, Pollard lovingly charts the wary gravitational pull between two orbiting loners, single high school teacher Carter Wagner (Sean O'Bryan) and transplanted New York veterinarian Maggie (Sybil Temchen). Carter is tired of being "just friends" with women he's attracted to, while Maggie is already sick and tired of the 'Southern Gentlemen' courtship rituals. While ever critical of matchmakers at work, Pollard's film plays matchmaker itself with considerable charm.

Whoa! Since when is a good-natured romantic comedy an independent film? In an era of indie popularity launched by the unexpected success of Steven Soderbergh's debut with the introspective *Sex, Lies and Videotape* (1989) — an era which arguably reached critical mass with the breakthrough boxoffice heat of Quentin Tarantino's ultra violent *Pulp Fiction* (1994) — *Nice Guys Sleep Alone* seems an aberration. Don't independent filmmaking require anger, outrage, an edge? When Edward Burns' *The Brothers McMullen* opened to critical praise and good boxoffice the same year *Pulp Fiction* surfaced, passionate indy filmmakers and aficionados dismissed Burns' easy-going chronicle of the relationship and romantic lives of the titular three siblings as being too lightweight for an independent film. In the half-decade since, diversity, not edge, characterizes the indie scene, and *Nice Guys Sleep Alone* wholeheartedly embraces both its independent pedigree and the romantic comedy tradition.

Stu Pollard came to filmmaking like most independent filmmakers: as a loner seeking an outlet for his creative urges. *"I spent a lot of time alone as a youngster,"* Stu recalls, *"so I was always looking for ways to amuse myself. As a teenager I started developing a big interest in sound."* This led to Stu working with *"a crappy cassette recorder, a crappy mixer from radio shack"* and borrowed tape decks to create his own audio productions. *"In my case, audio was the theater of the twisted mind,"* Stu says. *"So most of my high school classmates figured I'd end up in radio. I was the guy who announced the sports scores every morning over our school's PA system and DJed our dances. But my Dad changed all that in 1984, when he gave me a video camera for Christmas."*

Having nurtured his comedic and narrative skills with his crude audio productions, Stu quickly shifted gears to this new medium. *"Again, I had an almost voyeuristic fascination with recording things, only this time I was getting picture and sound,"* he recalls. *"I shot our entire antics-filled Spring Break, as well as quite a few scripted spots."* Stu continued refining his video skills during his college years at Georgetown University. *"Because it was mid-eighties, I was literally the only guy on campus with such a device. I got some priceless 'documentary style' footage that still provides good laughs to this day. I would imagine that if any of my college classmates ever decide to run for office, I'll get a call from them first."*

The limited editing capabilities of the medium in the mid-1980s frustrated Pollard's storytelling urge and derailed his momentum. *"I didn't do much of anything scripted, because any decent editing equipment was out of my financial reach. After I graduated, I actually gave the camera to my Mom and didn't shoot anything for two years."*

Thanks to a little help from his friends, Stu climbed back into the saddle. *"It was during that time that several of my college classmates said that I was swimming against my strength in the corporate world. They encouraged me to apply to film school; they even ordered applications for me. I applied and even though I had no portfolio to show — somehow I didn't think the admissions committees would have much interest in footage of some drunken fool guzzling beer from a flowerpot — I was accepted by USC, arguably the best film school in the country. And it was at USC Film School where my creative career path truly began."*

Stu's earlier film school productions paved the way for *Nice Guys* in more ways than one; one could argue that romantic comedy is Pollard's preferred genre. *"I made quite a few shorts in film school,"* Stu says, *"mostly on Super 8. They're OK, but what I'm most proud of are my wedding videos. Since 1992, I've made seven* Biography *type roasts. They usually consist of historical footage from college, present-day interviews with the groom's good friends, and skits that mock that groom's most telling (and usually sarcastically unappealing) traits."* Some of these productions were surprisingly elaborate. *"In* Wedlock and Load *(1997), the premise of the* Saturday Night Live-*ish opening skit was a Budweiser brewery strike that threatened to cancel the wedding. It was up to the groom's buddies to track down enough beer for the reception, and they soon found themselves in a bloody gun battle with the Bud-Weis-Er frogs."*

All this creative energy couldn't remain bottled up with such fare. *"As I finished up film school, I was sure of three things,"* Stu asserts. *"First, I wanted to make a feature film, rather than languish in school working on a short. I watched more than a few of my classmates pour six-figure sums into their thesis projects, which never made sense to me. If you're going to spend that kind of money, why not just make a feature? Second, I wanted to make a comedy; most likely a romantic one given my fascination with dating and relationships. And third, I needed something to make the project attractive to investors. As a first time filmmaker, I knew I needed something to make my project appear a little less risky. Basing the script on a best-selling book, Bruce Feirstein's* Nice Guys Sleep Alone, *turned out to be the answer."*

Adaptation from page to screen is always a tricky process, and Feirstein's bestseller provided its own unique challenges. Stu notes, *"*Nice Guys Sleep Alone *is not a novel. It's a book. And a very anecdotal one at that. 150 pages, 75 chapters."* Along with shaping Feirstein's episodic structure into a linear narrative, Pollard also had to localize his script. *"The book has nothing to do with Kentucky, Horse Racing, Horse Farms, English Teachers, Bourbon Drinking Millionaires, etc. It's the spirit of the book — 'there are only six people in this town, and they all know each other, so even if that person sitting across from you ain't right for you, maybe they'll know who is' — that most comes through in the movie. It was an incredibly difficult book to to adapt, and anyone else who tried to adapt it would come up with something very, very different. The best thing about the process was getting to work with Bruce Feirstein, who provided me a great deal of counsel along the way."*

That may have included a bit of legal counsel, too. *"The 'Pre-Relationship Agreement' was actually a chapter in the book,"* Stu chuckles, citing a mock-legal document in the film that also serves as a promotional item in savvy video stores currently racking Stu's feature. *"The tricky part was figuring out a way to transform it into something we could use in the film. The answer was creating the character of Slick Willie, the 'Relationship Attorney' who hawks his services, and the agreement, throughout the movie. Several other parts of the book became incorporated into dialogue."*

Once Pollard settled on his source material, he began scouting locations in his hometown of Louisville, Kentucky. *"There were three great things about shooting in Louisville,"* Stu says. *"It gave us a beautiful setting for our film. It was an incredibly supportive community: from street closures to extras to media coverage, we wanted for nothing thanks to the city's enthusiasm. As a first-timer, I couldn't have asked for a more film friendly environment. And finally, friends and family came through with locations. Just about every place we wanted to shoot, we were able to find a friend or relative who either had enough pull to get us the location, or knew someone else one who could. As I said, the community was supportive, and the locations we were able to secure are further proof of that."*

The casting process was even more important to the film. As Carter, lead player Sean O'Bryan essentially carries the film. *"I think Sean O'Bryan is the best thing about the film,"* Pollard says, *"he just completely nailed the part of Carter, and he was great to work with. As a first time director, I was very particular about not only working with good actors, but also working with nice people. Indie filmmaking is a team effort, with no room for prima donnas. One of the most appealing things about Sean is that he's very attractive, but not in the classical, tall, dark and handsome, square-jawed, ultra buff kind of way. Plenty of those types auditioned for Carter, and none of them were right. Who's going to believe some turbo handsome, zero body fat, chiseled Greek God is having woman troubles? Sean is perfect because — like Carter — he's someone who grows on you the more you get to know him. "*

Stu was not only fortunate to find an actor of such caliber, he lucked into one who comes across in the video and DVD extras as Stu's long-lost sibling... which isn't far from the truth. *"When Sean came in to audition, the first thing he told me was that he was from Louisville. Neither of us had any idea that we'd spent the better part of fifteen years growing up in the same town. Karma. Karma. Karma. After his first reading, I knew he had the part. As for his physical resemblance to me, well, I'd say that's more coincidence than any attempt at casting a surrogate version of myself. Yes, Carter is the character who most closely embraces my own life philosophies, but he's actually more idealistic than I am. All the characters in the film — men, women, nice, not-so-nice — reflect some portion of my makeup."*

Once completed, *Nice Guys Sleep Alone* faced the same gauntlet all independent features suffer. Luckily, Pollard's film has found its audience, via film festivals, limited theatrical release, and now home video. *"Our very first screening occurred at a film festival in Sweden before a packed house of 800 people. They loved it. We consistently sold out our festival screenings, which gave me the confidence to distribute the film theatrically myself. We got great reviews and were held over for multiple week runs in four of the five markets we played. We won Best of Fest at the Rhode Island International Festival; Best Comedy, Marco Island Film Fest; and Audience Award at the Las Vegas International Film Festival. On video, we were the top performing title in Hollywood Video's First Rites series with regards to number of turns: 8,000 copies rented 45,000 times during our six month exclusive. I've gotten great feedback on the video and DVD."*

When asked about his potential audience, Stu concludes that *"anyone who's ever dated will enjoy this film. I think those who will most identify with it are twenty and thirty somethings. It's been called 'The Perfect Date Movie' and certainly is a big hit with couples. It's a romantic comedy, but has a very masculine disposition to it."* Stu is overjoyed that *Nice Guys* has found its audience via video.

Discussing his future projects (including a TV series currently in development along with his next feature), Stu affirms the importance of the video market to his own future. *"Digital video means just about anyone can make something that would technically qualify as a feature. The internet means just about anything can be distributed. But this increase in quantity doesn't necessarily mean an increase in quality. There will always be video stores, and there will always be a number of independent films produced each year that are genuinely worthy of significant distribution. People will look to video stores to help them dig through the clutter. But no matter how big the internet gets, I think people will still want to cuddle up on their couch and watch a movie on their television. And they'll always want a living, breathing human to ask, 'What's new and good that I haven't seen?'"* For more information on *Nice Guys Sleep Alone*, go to: http://www.niceguysmovie.com[83]

April 5:

---

[83] Stu Pollard has kept busy since, having produced, directed and scripted *Keep Your Distance* (2005) and co-produced Robert Cary's romantic comedy *Ira and Abby* (2006), the documentary *Dirty Country* (2007) and Craig Johnson's *True Adolescents* (2008).

At first glance, ***THE LEGEND OF BAGGER VANCE*** and ***REMEMBER THE TITANS*** (both 2000) have nothing in common, really, other than shared noble aspirations, a firm belief in the dignity of the human spirit, and a focus on sports (golf in *Bagger*, football in *Titans*) as a measure of manhood. Sports offer a path to fulfilling one's abilities and, perhaps, transcending one's baser instincts (self-loathing and despair in *Bagger*, hatred and racism in *Titans*). Both films are impeccably crafted by studio standards and quite handsome, boasting top-drawer casts.

But take a closer look. Both features profer an African-American lead (Will Smith in *Bagger*, Denzel Washington in *Titans*) as the catalyst for victory against enormous odds and achieving the kind of redemption sports dramas revel in. There are similar story arcs — the lows of defeat and self-pity, the highs of the comeback and triumph — but ultimately, they are interesting companion features for the way they demonstrate how hard work and humility pays off (in Boaz Yakin's excellent *Remember the Titans*) and vanity betrays (in Robert Redford's pretentious *The Legend of Bagger Vance*).

The Legend of Bagger Vance is the golden boy here. 1990s 'golden boy' Matt Damon stars, under the direction of '60s and '70s 'golden boy' Redford; my, how the studios must have slavered over this match made in heaven. Redford, of course, embodied the beloved American archetype under consideration here when he played *The Natural* (1984), which was arguably Redford's last true 'movie star' turn. Redford guides Damon through similarly mythic byways (drawn from the novel by Steven Pressfield), adding the burden of

World War I to its hero's woes while supplanting the all-American sport of baseball with — ahem — golf. With its period setting and nostalgic luster, *Bagger Vance* comes across like a melancholy melange of *The Natural* by way of The *Great Gatsby* (1974) and *Legends of the Fall* (1994), garnished with a touch of *My Dog Skip* (2000; a mere lad, played by J. Michael Moncrief, plays a key role in Damon's reawakening).[84]

Shaken by his trench war experiences, once golden boy Rannulph Junuh (Damon) succumbs to misery and the bottle, abandoning his beloved Adele (Theron) and his magic on the green. Enter the mysterious caddy Bagger Vance (Will Smith) who guides Damon towards spiritual recovery and a comeback. With his folksy manner, rural zen wisdom, and almost preternatural abilities, Smith embodies the kind of character Scatman Crothers played in Steven Spielberg's sticky-sweet *"Kick the Can"* episode of *The Twilight Zone: The Movie* (1983). Redford and Smith don't quite stoop to that level of embarrassment, but it's nonetheless another racial stereotype: the African-American folk genie come to put the put-upon, once-rich white fool back on his feet and in touch with life itself, *if* he can get over his angst long enough to tune in to the magic (Stephen King's *The Green Mile*, 1999, recently embraced the archetype, too). Truth to tell, Vance is just a hoot and a holler from Disney's *"Zip-a-de-do-da"* Uncle Remus. Smith offers some levity, but Redford, Theron, and Damon play it like they're in church, somber as deacons. I could go on, but suffice to say *Bagger Vance* succumbs to the same turgid blend of fantasy and reality that characterized Redford's sophomore directorial effort *The Milagro*

---

[84] See *Blur, Vol. 2*, pp. 144-146.

Beanfield War (1988). Some found that film enchanting, but I found it tedious, and *Bagger Vance* is even less of a charmer.

Remember the Titans is everything *Bagger Vance* fails to be. No need for mysticism, magical caddies, or murky metaphors about life: *The Titans* forges its narrative out of the true-life trials and tribulations of Alexandria, Virginia's desegregated 1971 high school football team. The intrusion of African-American coach Herman Boone (Denzel Washington) into the team's all-white coaching staff and a bevy of black students into the ranks of the all-white team sets off the expected fireworks. The ire is further fueled by the resentment fostered by Boone's inadvertant demotion of coach Bill Yoast (Will Patton), which threatens Yoast's hard-earned bid to the football Hall of Fame. Racist strife splits the community, the team, the individuals and the families caught in this precarious moment of time, and it's up to Boone, Yoast, and the young players to navigate the treacherous minefield ahead.

Surely, we've been here before. On paper, *Titans* must have read like a TV movie, and a none-too-challenging one at that. As usual, historical truth was distorted to serve the expected narrative devices mainstream entertainment thrives upon. The film is even saddled with producer Jerry Bruckheimer's obligatory bogus males-bonding-singing-in-the-locker-room sequence[85] (come *on*, Jerry — enough is enough!). But screenwriter Gregory Allen Howard, director Boaz Ya-

---

[85] This seems to have originated with the pool table/barroom sequence in Michael Cimino's *The Deer Hunter* (1978) – and seems to be the *only* dramatic lesson Bruckheimer learned from that Academy-Award winner.

kin, costars Washington and Patton, and the ensemble young cast seize the day. Hoary story devices that shouldn't work — Yoast's feisty daughter, Boone's speech to the team amid the Gettysburg battlefield cemetary, the inevitable clash and bonding between the black and white team leaders — *do* work, because Howard, Yakin, and the players maintain a grace, gravity, and conviction that lends integrity and weight to the proceedings. Despite the ready recipe for formulaic Hollywood dross, *Remember the Titans* becomes an excellent film.

Then again, to my mind, Yakin is the better filmmaker here (his debut feature *Fresh*, 1994, remains one of the most moving American film experiences of the past decade), and Washington and Patton act circles around Damon and Smith. They, at least, have something more than cotton candy to sink their teeth into, and they do so with a purpose. Unlike Redford, Yakin confronts the very racism *Bagger Vance* indulges, in its coy 'politically-correct' way. More fundamentally, Yakin is in tune with day-to-day life and ordinary people under extraordinary circumstances in a way that infuses *Titans* with a believable ring of dignity and truth — the very ring that *Bagger Vance* fails to echo, much less capture, with its ponderous fantasy. Emulating the message of their film, *Titans'* cast and creators work hard to achieve their goals, despite the odds against them, and they succeed. *Titans* embodies the courage of its convictions; *Bagger* reflects the piety of its platitudes.

It's all in the titles, really. Forget *The Legend of Bagger Vance*; Remember *the Titans*. *(*Bagger Vance *is rated 'PG-13' for strong language, adult and sexual content, war violence;* Remember the Titans *is rated*

'PG' for strong language, sexual innuendo, mature content, and some violence.)

April 12:

In typical Hollywood fashion, last year found two very similar science fiction super-productions — Brian DePalma's *Mission to Mars* [86] and **RED PLANET** (2000), the debut feature from director Anthony Hoffman — racing each other to the boxoffice. *Red Planet* lost the boxoffice race, placing second with both opening date and boxoffice earnings, but it's by far the better of the two films. Though it's once again second out of the gate on home video, don't pass *Red Planet* by; it's well worth a look, particularly for sf fans.

Before I get anyone's hopes up, though, note that there's nothing particularly original going on here. Both *Red Planet* and *Mission to Mars* are throwbacks to 1950s and '60s-style science fiction gussied up with state-of-the-art casts and production values. DePalma's *Mission to Mars* was an enjoyable bit of a mishmash, a slick but uneasy wedding of "gee-whiz" George Pal '50s gadgetry with headier notions cribbed from Nigel Kneale (specifically *Quatermass and the Pit*, aka *Five Million Years to Earth*, originally produced as a BBC miniseries in 1958, Hammer Films adaptation 1967) by way of Arthur C. Clarke and Stanley Kubrick (*2001: A Space Odyssey*, natch; 1968), with a contemporary glaze of *The Right Stuff* (1983), *Apollo 13* (1995), and *Contact* (1997) to emulate fresh air. *Red Planet* eschews such pretensions for a straight-forward survival tale, and it's all the better for it. If I had to cite specific cinematic

---

[86] See *Blur, Vol. 2*, pp. 203-204.

predecessors (there are too many literary sf godfathers to list here), Kurt Neumann's *Rocketship X-M* (1951) and Byron Haskin's *Robinson Crusoe on Mars* (1963) would take the honors. The latter film by Haskins (who also directed the 1953 *War of the Worlds*, among others) was a colorful sleeper that honorably adapted Daniel Defoe's classic to the space age, and *Red Planet* hews to that film's modest example. This is a survival tale, pure and simple, with an imaginative enough set-up (the bio-engineering of Mars for possible colonization) and probable enough flora (bio-engineered algae) and fauna (indigenous Martian insects that swarm and feed) to offset it's hokier elements (ah, thank God —there's oxygen on Mars!).

Red Planet's nominal hero, played by Val Kilmer, doesn't have *Robinson Crusoe on Mars*' Mona the monkey for companionship, but then again, he isn't really alone on the inhospitable, barren world. There's a clutch of crewmembers who survive the crash-landing (Terence Stamp, Tom Sizemore, Benjamin Bratt, Simon Baker), and a lovely mission commander Bowman (the name a nod to *2001*, the character played by Carrie-Anne Moss from *The Matrix*, 1999[87]) orbiting overhead. Bowman might manage an against-all-odds rescue, if they're able to somehow reach the ship before the dwindling fuel and narrowing launch window leaves them forever stranded on Mars.

Oh, yes, and there's AMEE, an ambulatory, autonomous explorative robot who suffers a blow to the virtual skull during landing and thus becomes a bosom sibling of *2001*'s homicidal HAL-9000 (and the countless rampaging robots before and after HAL, arguably

---

[87] See *Blur, Vol. 1*, pp. 51-53.

most like the lethal lunar composite war machine in the forgotten *Moontrap*, 1989). Since *Red Planet* eschews the usual Martian monsters and menaces (save for the tiny swarming invertebrates I mentioned earlier), AMEE assumes the role of demonic other, sliding into lethal military mode and bristling with razors to fine-tune her high-tech tracking skills by taking out the survivors, one by one.

There's nothing particularly outstanding here, but the cast plays it straight (with Sizemore the standout), the script is efficient and engaging, fledgling director Anthony Hoffman keeps the pace tight and storytelling appropriately lean, and the special effects are excellent throughout. Keep your expectations in check, oxygen on, and go for the ride. My son and I had a fine time with it, and hope you will, too. *(Rated 'PG-13' for partial nudity, language, and some graphic violence.)*

There's no questioning the passion and integrity of ***MEN OF HONOR*** (2000), a solid military drama drawn from the life of the first African-American U. S. Navy diver Carl Brashear (Cuba Gooding, Jr.), but the film falls short of its aspirations. It is also the story of Brashear's primary mentor and nemesis, Master Chief Billy Sunday (Robert De Niro), whose hatred of Brashear's color, spirit, and perseverence is sanctioned by the obsessive command of diving school C.O. 'Mister Pappy' (Hal Holbrook, looking more like 1950s character actor Morris Ankrum with every role).

With stoic determination, director George Tillman, Jr. efficiently navigates this often-harrowing account of Brashear's tenacity in the face of institutionalized racism and brutality. Unfortunately, Tillman and the fine cast are saddled with an episodic, clumsily structured screenplay that lurches rather than flows through Brashear's story with dogmatic, unimaginative drive. Spanning a quarter-of-a-century (1943-68), by leaving too many gaps of time, events, and most of all characterization the script ill-serves Brashear's saga.

Typical of the genre, the female characters (Aunjanue Ellis as Brashear's love Jo, Charlize Theron as Sunday's young wife Gwen) are mere ciphers, longsuffering military wives fretting over their bull-headed men. Gender isn't the issue, though: the male characters have little depth, either. In the simplistic determinism of this telling, Brashear is driven by his love and devotion to his sharecropper father (Carl Lumbly); however, Brashear's relationship with his own son and family is less than an onscreen whisper, much to the detriment of the film's primary theme. Sunday is a cornpone brute, a vehicle for yet another monstrous De Niro father figure (which he memorably defined in *This Boy's Life*, 1993, and recently parodied in *Meet the Parents*, 2000); De Niro brings his usual fire to the role, but the script provides little more than a caricature to inhabit.

In the end, the film is as much about how the military breaks *and* 'makes' men as it is about Brashear's indomitable refusal to yield to blind racism and prejudice. Like most of today's military sagas (from *A Few Good Men*, 1992, to *Rules of Engagement*, 2000), *Men of Honor* concludes in a courtroom: in a final act of ritualized sadism, the conflict between 'Old Navy' and 'New Navy' is put to the test along with Brashear's (and Sunday's) career.[88] Again, the maladroit script falters,

---

[88] The grand archetype of this contemporary model is, of course, Herman Wouk's novel *The Caine Mutiny*, filmed in 1954 and 1988.

skirting volatile emotional issues (Jo's seperation from Brashear when he choses his career over family) while asking us to side with the 'Old Navy.' Brashear's devotion to 'Old Navy' traditions stands tall, but we've precious little sympathy left for the institution's sense of 'honor' the film romanticizes after two hours of 'Old Navy' attempts to strip-mine Brashear and others with good ol' boy emotional, psychological, and physical savagery. Thanks only to Cuba Gooding, Jr.'s performance our sympathies remain aligned with Brashear, the man, to the bitter end.

Despite the muddled vehicle, Gooding, Jr. carries the day and makes *Men of Honor* worth a viewing. The recent *Remember the Titans* offers a far more intelligent and focused dramatization of racial conflict and victory over prejudice, but I've no doubt that most veterans and old sea dogs will find *Men of Honor* an irresistable rental. *(Rated 'R' for strong language, military brutality, violence, adult content.)*

April 19:

BAMBOOZLED (2000) is Spike Lee's latest joint, a timely attack on media racism, past, present, and future. Reacting to plummeting ratings, CNS corporate executive Dunwitty (Michael Rapaport) embraces a mocking series premise proposed by the network's only black writer, Pierre Delacroix (Damon Wayans of *Living Color*, 1990-94, *I'm Gonna Get You Sucka*, 1988, *Mo' Money*, 1992, etc.). Inspired by the unlikely fusion of old *Amos and Andy* clips and a recent sidewalk encounter with homeless street dancers Manray (Savion Glover) and Womack (Tommy Davidson), Delacroix brainstorms an insulting blackface variety revue entitled *Mantan, The*

New Millennium Minstrel Show, featuring Manray as Mantan and Womack as 'Sleep'n'Eat,' a pair of *"ignorant, dull-witted, lazy, and unlucky"* caricatures. As in *The Producers* (1968) and (closer to Lee's turf) *Network* (1976), Delacroix's brainchild (*"a family show that takes place in a watermelon patch"*) becomes a wild success, spinning Lee's conceit into multi-layered dissections of racist stereotypes, archetypes, and entertainments.

Bamboozled is Lee's reactionary satire of an American underbelly he finds increasingly suspect and intolerable: young white culture's embrace of black culture; contemporary permutations of black pop culture Lee and others consider self-destructive; archaic racist and racial stereotypes (from 1940s black actors like Mantan Moreland and Stepin Fetchit to 1970s TV series like *The Jeffersons* and *Good Times*) that maintain their hold through misplaced nostalgia. As such, the film is an angry companion piece and comeback to the Gangsta scene, films like James Toback's *Black and White* (1999), and Quentin Tarantino's much-publicized misbehavior (and addictive use of the 'n' word in his screenplays), though there's plenty of racism evident in other forms in contemporary culture (including films that pretend to address the issue while embracing archetypes: *The Green Mile, The Legend of Bagger Vance, Men of Honor*, etc.).

Choosing to film on video and Super 16mm to capture a non-Hollywood immediacy throughout, Lee stokes the first half of the film like a furnace. Initially, the result is gripping, brutally funny, and strangely personal. The spectacle of Manray tap-dancing for Dunwitty palpably embodies Lee's frustrations with pitching projects to pandering Hollywood executives, just as Delacroix's weary reaction to an assaultive rap performance during auditions (*"I don't want anything to do with anything black for at least a week"*) succinctly summarizes Lee's oft-stated objections to much of the current music scene.

But the uneven tone and increasingly derivative debt to Paddy Chayevsky's scathing *Network* take a toll. *Bamboozled* loses its focus long before the guns blaze in the extended climax, the last desperate act of an angry, fertile creator who's written himself into a corner. Horror of horrors, we find our attention wandering from his characters' dire plight to the fascinating collection of racist artifacts the set decorators cobbled together; surely, this wasn't the filmmaker's intent. At 136 minutes, *Bamboozled* wears out its welcome before Lee intends it to, but it's still a provocative effort, well worth a look — particularly on DVD, where Lee's running commentary proves ultimately more engaging, illuminating, and memorable than his creation. *(Rated 'R' for strong language, violence, gunplay, alcohol and drug use and abuse, racist and adult content.)*

Ethan Hawke's star turn as ***HAMLET*** (2000) boasts the ugliest hat of the year, crowning the young (corporate) prince's perpetually unwashed hair like a filthy parking meter cover. But don't judge this Hamlet by his (ahem) cover.

At first glance, there's plenty else to put off Shakespeare afficianados. Herein, *"one woe doth tread upon another's heels"* in the Big Apple, circa 2000 A.D.. Denmark is a Manhattan-based corporation, its castles are sterile steel and glass skyscrapers and offices. Gone is the famed graveside speech, here glimpsed fleetingly on a television monitor (as an excerpt from an earlier cinematic Shakespeare adaptation) — but we do spot the gravedigger singing *"All Along the Watchtower."* The other major soliloqueys are intact: *"To be, or not to be"* is delivered as a video playback; *"To die, perchance to dream"* graces the aisles of a Blockbuster video store; *"what is a man"* darkens the confines of a jet airliner. Rosencrantz and Guilderstern (Steve Zahn and Dechen Thurman) deliver their covert observations of Hamlet's odd behavior via speakerphone; *"the commission"* commanding the prince's death malingers on a laptop; Hamlet announces his impending return via FAX. Here, the tragic Ophelia (Julia Stiles) wears a wire and her breakdown shakes the Guggenheim gallery, while the performance Hamlet stages to test his suspicions of his newlywed stepfather (Kyle MacLachlan) and mother (Diane Venora) is a digitally-produced underground film of his own making. Images of James Dean and the Crow flicker on screens like resurrected spirits, and to my knowledge this is the first and only intepretation of Shakespeare's venerable tragedy to accompany the first visitation of the ghost of Hamlet's father (Sam Shepard) with a Pepsi product placement.

Revisionist cinematic Shakespeare adaptations are nothing new these days. Tanks rolled through the facist Art Deco 1930s London of Richard Loncraine's *Richard III* (1995); handguns and gang wars riddled Baz Luhrmann's Leonardo DiCaprio/Claire Danes version of *William Shakespeare's Romeo + Juliet* (1996); the recent *Titus* (2000) meshed faux Rome with anachronistic contemporary flourishes.[89] The trend continues with director Michael Almereyda's *Hamlet*, the filmmaker's fourth and best film (preceded by the akimbo *Twister*,

---

[89] See *Blur, Vol. 2*, pp. 189-203.

1989, and his new age spins on *Dracula* and *The Mummy* in *Nadja*, 1995, and *The Eternal*, 1999). What's next? Macbeth bloodying Florida theme parks to claim his throne there, 'til 'Disney Woods' advance upon Universal Studios' thrill rides?

If it's as engaging as Almereyda's *Hamlet*, I'll be the first in line. This inventive adaptation of *Hamlet* is surprisingly good, and true to the Bard in content and context. It succeeds marvelously thanks to a coherent vision and surprisingly strong performances throughout (including a fine turn by Bill Murray). Recommended! *(Rated 'R' for graphic violence, adult content, and casual drug and alcohol use.)*

A warning to the young, a recommendation to the old: whippersnappers will find Clint Eastwood's latest concoction a crashing bore, while old-timers will find it a real hoot. It's just that simple, really. Clearly building on Senator John Glenn's successful return to orbit, ***SPACE COWBOYS*** (2000) contrives to launch Eastwood (as ever, acting his age), Tommy Lee Jones, James Garner, and Donald Sutherland beyond the stratosphere to deal with a crumbling Soviet satellite suspiciously dependent upon stolen American operating systems. For reasons I won't give away here (the plot is too thin to betray), said Russkie satellite can't be allowed to simply burn up in the Earth's atmosphere, just as Eastwood and company can't be permitted to gracefully retire.

This is a slight, pleasant diversion, but as I say, it's not for the tykes. Those of us over forty will find much to savor here from the veteran cast and their respective methods of dealing with outdated attitudes and the stubborn flesh. My sweetie (who's a big James Garner fan) and I had a fine time, and I particularly enjoyed seeing

Eastwood and Sutherland back on the screen three decades after *Kelly's Heroes* (1970). Eastwood plays and directs with his usual steady hand, delivering a slick, amusing evening's entertainment of little consequence. But I've yet to find anyone twenty-five or younger who didn't walk out of the theater or just turn off the television. Ha! The joke's on them. Ten or twenty years from now, they *will* get it... and Clint and company will be dancing on their graves, won't they? *Eeeeeeee*-hah! *(Rated 'PG-13' for language, partial nudity, and some sexual content.)*

April 26th:

FINDING FORRESTER (2000) was a real favorite here in town during its theatrical run at the Latchis, and it's easy to see why. South Bronx high school student Jamal (Robert Brown) maintains his toehold among friends and community with his basketball skills, but he has a secret: he is a gifted writer. Above the neighborhood hoop court, a strange white man known only as *"The Window"* gazes down with binoculars; when Jamal accepts the dare to break into *"The Window"* apartment, he is startled and flees, leaving his backpack and writing notebook behind. *"The Window"* finds, reads, and edits the intruder's notebook before returning it, and so begins the relationship between Jamal and the hermit who once one a Pulitzer Prize for his one and only novel, published four decades before.

Sean Connery co-stars as the enigmatic William Forrester — 'The Window' — who incarnates his nickname with the sort of literalism these kinds of tales thrive upon. Forrester becomes Jamal's window to a new life as a writer, while Jamal becomes Forrester window to the world he turned his back on forty years ago. The blossoming of their tenuous relationship, its flowering into a fuller life for men who've each invested so much into hiding their skills beneath layers of armor, is the story here, and the ensemble cast skillfully inhabits the tale under the steady guidance of director Gus Van Sant, whose become an old hand at this peculiar genre since scoring big with *Good Will Hunting* (1997).

The question, though, is whether we should be trying to Find Van Sant: are these films representative of a gifted filmmaker finding his muse at last, or burying his talents beneath a commercially-viable formula, just as Forrester and Jamal bury their lights beneath the redstones of the South Bronx until they find each other? Prior to *Good Will Hunting*, Van Sant made his mark with a restless, sometimes caustic street-life cinema that embraced the American underbelly with a passion and clarity that was distinctively his own: *Drugstore Cowboy* (1989), *My Own Private Idaho* (1991), and *To Die For* (1995) were (and remain) extraordinary films. Then again, there was the misfire of *Even Cowgirls Get the Blues* (1994), then came the Hanson video and the incredibly unnecessary remake of Alfred Hitchcock's *Psycho* (1998) — as suffocating and sterile a piece of work as one could imagine for a director like Van Sant — with the populist *Good Will Hunting* alone rising above the context of such rootless meanderings. *Finding Forrester* builds upon the very strengths that made *Good Will Hunting* such a hit (including a cameo from Matt Damon, as if the lad were a good luck charm), and though it does find and maintain its own footing, one cannot help but wonder if Van Sant is retreating to what has become safe, familiar turf.

As a comforting, engaging evening entertainment, I enjoyed *Finding Forrester* as much as the rest of Brattleboro. There's no denying Van Sant's skillful handling of such material, capturing the street, the halls of academia, and the inner lives of his characters with persuasive finesse. Connery inhabits Forrester with a vigor precious few of his more recent roles affords, and that, too, is engaging. But the ease with which this cozy formula (and it is a formula) goes down is troubling, making me long for the kind of daring, fearless, sometimes abrasively reckless films Van Sant once helmed. If this is Van Sant's *"Window,"* so be it; if it isn't, though, here's hoping he loses his backpack in the right apartment soon.[90] *(Rated 'PG-13' for strong language, some adult content.)*

The title **TIGERLAND** (2000) refers to *"the second worst place on earth,"* a military training camp in Florida that's the last stop for recruits en route to Vietnam, designed to simulate what awaits the grunts in Asia. The year is 1971, the primary setting Fort Polk, where the ridiculously young recruits of A-company, second platoon are put through their basic training paces to prepare them for Tigerland and the seemingly-inevitable hell of Vietnam thereafter.

Among the platoon of raw rednecks, idealists, saps, and borderline psychos is Texan loner Roland Bozz

---

[90] With his next feature, the enigmatic *Gerry* (2002), Van Sant returned to his roots with far more personal films, followed by *Elephant* (2003), *Last Days* (2005) and *Paranoid Park* (2007), as well as various short film and music videos. None were popular, but all are worth seeing and far more compelling to cinéastes than *Finding Forrester*.

(Colin Farrell), who's at war with the military establishment. Determined to derail the speed-track to Tigerland and the 'Nam for himself and as many fellow grunts as possible, Bozz has spent the majority of his three months in training locked up in the stockade for various infractions. His C.O. (Nick Searcy) is determined to break Bozz, but the Texan perpetually thinks and acts outside the envelope (managing honorable discharges for the privates he considers too weak or strained to survive); Bozz's motives, though, are his own, despite the best efforts of his one friend, Jim Paxton (Matt Davis), and his C.O. to decipher the Texan's decidedly mixed signals. Refusing to participate in or accept the psychological and physical brutality that's basic's 'business as usual,' Bozz sparks the ire of an increasingly violent recruit (Shea Whigham) eager to tear Bozz down to size by any means necessary. Down the road, Tigerland looms, ever closer...

This excellent military drama is based on the experiences of co-screenwriter Ross Klavan (represented by the character of Paxton), and the authenticity of place, time, and tenor is exhilerating. This tale of damnation and redemption is also a redemptive effort from Hollywood hack Joel Schumacher, who scraped bottom with his slick, empty direction of dross like *8MM* (1999) and (choke) *Batman & Robin* (1997). Determined to reengage with his fundamental love for cinema, Schumacher embraced elements of the European Dogma 95 manifesto,[91] stripping his techniques down to the bare minimum (handheld cameras, no special effects, etc.) to make the finest film of his career. This isn't the first war film of its kind — Patrick Duncan's underrated, forgot-

---

[91] See the final essay in this volume for more on Dogme 95.

ten *84 Charlie Mopic* (1989) made potent use of similar *"you are are"* versimilitude before Dogma 95 was even a gleam in Lars Von Triers' eye — but *Tigerland* is a remarkable film, skirting the usual glib cliches of the genre to dig for deeper truths. Colin Farrell is riveting, delivering one of the year's finest performances. Not to be missed! *(Rated 'R' for strong language, male nudity, sexual situations, gunplay, psychological sadism, and war violence.)*

April 26: Indie Comedy **WAITING** *is "60% Autobiographical, 40% Lies"*

It's rare that an independently made comedy feature hits a shared cultural nerve as soundly as writer/director Patrick Hasson's ***WAITING*** (2000).[92] Anyone frustrated with the minimum-wage work scene (and the after-hours dating scene) will find plenty to amuse in *Waiting* — which, like many great comedic works, was borne out of its creator's sheer agony.

"Waiting *was the culmination of eight years of pain I endured working in the restaurant industry,"* the young Philadelphian filmmaker tells us. Well, maybe it wasn't all agony: *"The fast woman and quick cash did help to feed the nasty filmmaking habit I've picked up over the years,"* Patrick admits.

Thankfully, the fruits of that *"filmmaking habit"* are highly entertaining. All in all, the comedy feature emerged from four years of hard work (and waiting ta-

---

[92] Well, OK, Kevin Smith's *Clerks* (1994) counts, *big* time, and was undoubtably the inspiration for *Waiting* – but for the purposes of this interview/article, I chose to focus on Patrick's film outside of that sizeable shadow.

bles). *"I began taking notes in 1996 during one of my stints as a waiter,"* Patrick says. *"By 1997, I had filled up enough napkins, checks, and receipts with ideas to begin writing the script. By 1998, the script was completed. In April of 1999, we shot the film over four weeks, the editing took eight months, and* Waiting *had its first screening in January of 2000."* And the rest, as they say, is history in the making.

Waiting is narrated by put-upon college grad Sean McNutt (Will Keenan of *Tromeo and Juliet* and *Terror Firmer*), whose father has delivered an ultimatum: Sean has just thirty days to get out of the old homestead and find his own apartment. Of course, Sean's already deep in debt, and his latest dead-end job — waiting tables at Broccoletti's, a South Philadelphia Italian bistro — barely pays enough to make such a move possible. Sean is also addled by his ongoing attempts to patch things up with his ex-girlfriend Andrea (Kerri Kenney), though she's currently dating a lout who delights in tormenting Sean at every turn.

Writer/director Hasson and producer John Stefanic mount an affectionate, infectious insider's peek at the restaurant work scene sure to delight and disgust viewers (while prompting more than a few worries about one's next dining experience). When asked how much of *Waiting* is autobiographical, Patrick confesses, *"60% autobiographical, 40% lies. My advice to all those waiting tables: don't sleep with the hostess (or host) if you want to sit more than one table a night."*

The bulk of *Waiting* is set in Broccoletti's, where Sean and his fellow underpaid co-workers fume at the customers, each other, and squeeze all they can out of their inebriated midnight-to-dawn search for a good time. Fortunately, John Stefanic stumbled upon an ideal location in Philadelphia for the intensive one-month shoot. *"I had worked freelance for the last three years doing locations in film industry,"* John says, noting that finding the locations *"was one of the easier parts"* of his producer chores. *"A good friend of mine, Patricia Taggart, is a location manager in Philly and she helped also. As far as the restaurant goes, it was a bit of luck. The place literally around the corner from me closed their upstairs restaurant (the downstairs bar was still open) a month before we went into principle photography. I knew the people pretty well and it all worked out. The restaurant is actual."*

The core of the film, however, is Patrick's surrogate self, Sean McNutt. In another stroke of good fortune, Patrick and John found the perfect leading man for their saga in Will Keenan, who the *Hollywood Reporter* recently touted as *"the hardest working actor at Sundance."* Though Keenan is still a young actor, he's already cut his teeth in over twenty-five independent features, including lead roles in Troma's *Tromeo and Juliet* (his debut feature, 1996) and *Terror Firmer* (1999) and non-Troma opuses like *Love God* (1997), *Trick* (1999), *The Love Machine* (2000), *Margarita Happy Hour* (2001), *Operation Midnight Climax* (2002), the just-completed *The Man Who Would Be King: The Benny Mardones Story*. [93]

---

[93] This last film was apparently never released; Will also appeared in *A.K.A.: It's a Wiley World!* (2003), *Alice's Misadventures in Wonderland, Love Room* (both 2004), *Shooting Vegetarians*, (2005), *Wicked Lake* (2008), *The Ghastly Love of Johnny X* (2009), and co-scripted, co-directed and starred in the short *Mission Accomplished Man!* (2006). Will cofounded Hoverground Studios and Go-Kart Films in 2003-2004, nur-

"Patrick saw him in Love God, *sent him a script and he came down to read,"* John recalls. *"Will as the lead was easy, he had the charisma to carry the movie. That was the hard part, knowing we had to find somebody who could pull it off. Sean McNutt is on the screen 75 out of the 80 minutes."*

Patrick adds, *"I went to see a screening of* Love God *with a friend* [Stefan Avalos, director of *The Money Game* and co-director of *The Last Broadcast*] *in Philly. Will plays the schizophrenic lead of the film and his performance absolutely blew me away. He did things I had never seen on the screen before, so I thought, 'this could be the McNutt I'm looking for.' Will was in attendance at the screening and Stefan introduced us afterwards. I told Will about* Waiting, *sent him a script a few weeks later, he dug it, and the rest is total perversion."*

Indeed. The sex-capades in *Waiting* are lively fun, peppered with a free-for-all evening of couplings between the after-hours staff that's abruptly terminated by a misplaced corkscrew. There's also the opportunistic revenge exacted by one of Sean's dominatrix ex-girlfriends that sends Sean, leather-masked and almost nude, scurrying into the streets of Philadelphia.

When asked if these antics were improvised, John says, *"Will had a lot of ideas and Patrick was receptive."* Patrick confirms this, adding, *"the film is about 80% straight off the script, but the rest is the comedic chaos of Mr. Keenan et al. Will really took the film to another level with his physical comedy and impeccable sense of timing. His willingness to take chances — eat-*

---

turing wide distribution (via Koch) for his own projects and those of many other filmmakers; for more information, go to http://www.gokartfilms.com

ing shaving cream, running through rush hour traffic half-naked, etc. — really had an effect on all the performances. His energy was addictive and I think the whole cast fed off it."

Some of Keenan's high-octane performance didn't make the final cut. John notes, *"Patrick's shooting ratio was 25 to 1. So we have hours upon hours of footage that didn't make the grade."* Patrick adds, *"you'll just have to wait for the DVD...it'll all be there."*

Keenan won a Best Actor Award for his efforts from the Williamsburg Brooklyn Film Festival. Whether he's spurning the advances of the diapered middle-aged *"Baby Poo Poo"* or spraying shaving cream into his mouth to clear his alcohol-tainted breath before the cops pull him over, Keenan carries the film with style to spare.

"Will did *eat the shaving cream,"* Patrick says. *"In fact, Will picked up quite a nasty habit after we filmed that scene, finding him several times huddled in a corner huffing cream, foaming at the mouth...as you can imagine, it was a pretty ugly scene. We were able to get him into a detox program and keep him out of the press until shooting was over. I have to be honest with you, a lot of the scandal-esque stuff that happened on set I'm not at liberty to disclose due to its involvement with the Bush daughters (lets just say they haven't been to confession in a while)."* Ah, okay, Patrick (I can't share the rest of his reveries in a family newspaper).

Somehow, John's version of events seems a bit more believable. *"Yes, Will did eat the shaving cream!,"* John says. *"I think our craziest event, though, was doing a publicity stunt for the Philly Premier: Will dressed in the bug suit scaled a 6 or 7 story water tower. I was calling all the news stations reporting a large green bug on the Connelly Water tower hanging a flyers banner. Three news helicopters and five police cars later, we were handcuffed in the back of separate police cars. I was talking to the officer in charge (stilled cuffed in the back of the car), when I noticed the officers took Will out of the car, uncuffed him, pulled the crime scene Polaroid out of the trunk and started taking pictures with him. Apparently, they recognized Will and decided to make it a photo-op. So there I am, still cuffed in the back of a police car, pleading our case, and Will is giving autographed pictures to the arresting officers. We had to go to court for disorderly conduct but the judge dropped all the charges."*

Luckily, not all the opening nights were so traumatic. "Waiting *debuted at the No Dance Film Festival 2000 in Park City, Utah,"* Patrick proudly says. *"The film won the Audience Award for Best Feature."* In fact, *Waiting* has earned three Audience Awards for Best Feature (NoDance, San Francisco, Williamsburg Brooklyn). *"The film has screened at over twenty film festivals worldwide,"* Patrick adds, *"and had limited theatrical runs in New York and Philadelphia."*

For the video release of *Waiting*, Patrick and John stuck to their indy guns, self-producing and self-distributing their feature. *"The deals that were coming our way just weren't all that lucrative and we felt we could do a better job on our own,"* Patrick says. *"The response has been phenomenal and more copies are going out each day."* John adds, *"It seems that you draw more attention and people want to get involved when you do it yourself. I believe we will hit the audience the film deserves."* Such success does, however, attract industry attention: *"We are very close to signing a video deal with a label,"* John concludes. This can only bring *Waiting* to a wider audience.

The ongoing promotion and self-distribution of *Waiting* occupies much of Patrick and John's efforts, but neither is ready to rest on their laurels. John is negotiating with *Hot Rod Magazine*, hoping to document the magazine's upcoming 2001 Power Tour. *"Basically, hundreds of hot rods drive from one point in the country to another point, stopping in a different state for a different car show everyday for ten days. This year, for the 75th anniversary of Route 66, they're going down the 'mother road'."* John intends to be there, preserving the event on film.[94]

For Patrick (who had already completed one feature prior to *Waiting*[95]), other projects beckon. *"I am currently writing three new feature scripts — two comedies and a horror flick, one of which might star Will Keenan with a full-on mullet — and beginning to seek financing for the projects. I'm also working on a few digital shorts under my new umbrella, No Head Films."*

In the meantime, what are you *Waiting* for? Check out *Waiting*, now available at your local independent video store, for a high time and a lively evening's dining experience.[96]

---

[94] John Stefanic completed *American Hot Rod: The Unauthorized Power Tour Documentary* (2004, see http://www.americanhotrod.tv) and produced Lance Weiler's *Head Trauma* (2006).

[95] *The Speed of Mind*, 1997.

[96] Patrick Hasson subsequently wrote, directed and edited the short film *Dead Broke* (2004), and has completed the feature *Mr. Patrick & the Hollywood Stars* (2007); see http://www.patrickhasson.com. A film entitled *Waiting...* by writer/director Rob McKittrick was released to mainstream

May 3-10: DOGMA 95: Of Donkey-Boys and Dancers

The first image — a signed full-screen certificate — of Harmony Korine's latest feature *JULIEN DONKEY-BOY* (1999) guarantees that Korine's feature was produced in strict accord with the 'Dogma 95' Manifesto. It looks awfully official, though such authoritarian pretensions are an anathema to the Dogma 95 founders and practitioners. In accord with the roughshod Dogma 95 aesthetic, this certificate is the only thing that looks officious about *Julien Donkey-Boy*.

But *who* is this certificate intended for? What does it mean? Why should we care? Whether you know it or not, the impact of the Dogma 95 movement is already being felt in mainstream American cinema.

Briefly: the Dogma 95 manifesto was founded in (duh) 1995 by a clutch of angry, ambitious Danish and Scandinavian directors who rejected completely the artifice of 1990s studio filmmaking. In short, Dogma 95 aimed to strip contemporary cinema to a more immediate, primal essence. Features were to be filmed with

---

venues in 2005, and was strikingly similar to *Waiting*. Online promotion and sources (including imdb.com postings by McKittrick) deny any association with Hasson and Stefanic's film: on August 27, 2005, McKittrick wrote, *"I can assure you, it's not a ripoff of the Will Keenan film. I wrote it back in '97 (and have the writer's guild registration and copyright to prove it), a couple years before the Hasson film came out..."* (http://www.imdb.com/title/tt0348333/board/thread/25188705?d=25191723#25191723). Patrick Hasson has posted his side of the controversy – which has uncanny ties to the *Last Broadcast/Blair Witch Project* controversy — at http://www.patrickhasson.com/?page_id=15, which provides ample links if you care to know more.

handheld cameras shooting with available light, preferably in 'real time.' Eschewing theatrical narrative convention, the rigorously controlled and contrived creation of false realities for the camera, studio gloss, and any special effects for a "you are there" sense of immediacy and essential 'reality,' key Dogma 95 practitioners like Danish director Lars Von Trier (*Breaking the Waves*, 1996; *The Idiots/Idioterne*, 1998, etc.) and Thomas Vinterberg (*The Celebration/Festen*, 1998) forged a brave new path opposed to the live-action cartoons that dominated mainstream theaters across the globe.

As an aesthetic built upon a reactionary backlash against the "anything goes" CGI-gloss of international big-budget films, Dogma 95 was in fact a fresh adoption of the very *cinéma vérité* techniques pioneer documentary filmmakers and independent directors associated with the silent era's Russian *Kino-Pravda* (literally, 'cinema of truth') and particularly the French New Wave — Francois Truffaut, Jean-Luc Godard, etc. – adopted in the late 1950s, fueling the seminal works of early '60s American directors like John Cassavetes and Shirley Clarke. Adapting the stripped-down approach documentary filmmakers like Richard Leacock and D.A. Pebbebaker to narrative film, Truffaut and Godard shot on the streets and engaged with a form of naturalism new to European cinema, while Cassavetes (*Shadows*, 1960) and Clarke (*The Connection*, 1962, *The Cool World*, 1964, etc.) indulged improvisational performances (or, at its finest, non-performances) in hopes of capturing lightening in a lens: all sought to redefine cinema via the look, feel, passion, fire of life itself. With his directorial debut feature *Shadows*, Cassavetes made the approach his own, refining it to an art in films like *Faces* (1968), *Husbands* (1970), *A Woman Under the Influence*

(1974), and others. The aesthetic's roots in the documentary form also shaped the 1960s generation of documentarians, led by filmmakers like the Maysles Brothers and Frederick Wiseman.

This approach to filmmaking thrived under a variety of monikers — *cinéma vérité,* 'free cinema,' 'Direct Cinema,' etc. – and adopted some of the conventions of movie newsreels and television news. This orientation currently informs the current wave of sensationalistic "reality TV" fodder from *Cops* to *Survivor* — which, perversely, shadows the Dogma 95 movement even as it trivializes its aesthetic. Even horror, science fiction and speculative 'what if?' narrative movies quickly adopted the techniques of *cinéma vérité*, as evidenced by John Frankenheimer's *Seven Days in May* (1964), Peter Watkin's *The War Game* (1967), and George Romero's *Night of the Living Dead* (1968). It's interesting to note that Wiseman's seminal portrait of a Massachusetts mental institution in *Titicut Follies* (1967) was recently pirated wholesale for *The Blair Witch Project* video spinoff, *The Burkittsville 7* (2000).[97] Note, too, that *The Blair Witch Project* was a streamlined adoption and exploitation of the Dogma 95 manifesto, though Von Trier had already completed the form's most ambitious horror masterpiece with *The Kingdom* (*Riget*, 1994) and *The Kingdom II* (*Riget II*, 1997).

As I noted in last week's review of Joel Schumacher's excellent new feature *Tigerland*, prominent Hollywood players are embracing the Dogma 95 agenda as a redemptive tool, if you will. If any contemporary filmmaker embodies the worst of Hollywood's fabled excesses, a case could be made for Schumacher, who

---

[97] See *Blur, Vol. 1*, pp. 85-88.

alienated even the most undemanding, braindead mainstream viewers with the mindlessly bloated emptiness of *Batman & Robin* (1997), a film that was literally *all* artifice. Intent on reaffirming his skills and his own love for cinema, Schumacher's stripped-down approach to the Vietnam-era bootcamp experiences of *Tigerland* yielded his best work to date, and curiously echoes another precursor to the Dogma 95 movement, the sadly neglected Vietnam drama *84 Charlie Mopic* (1989).

But the most prominent American adherent of the Dogma 95 manifesto is young upstart Harmony Korine. Since his debut, Korine's path has been strangely intertwined with the Dogma 95 circuit: at age 19, Korine scandalized America with his unflinching screenplay for Larry Clark's *Kids* the very year the Dogma 95 manifesto was drafted. Korine and Clark's scathing, sexually-explicit snapshot of 24 hours of contemporary urban teen life set the stage for Korine's directorial debut feature *Gummo* (1997), a less harrowing but nonetheless disturbing companion piece to *Kids* depicting a suburban dead-end juvenile limbo. Korine peppered nihilistic portrait of a bleak existence in Ohio with random mayhem, eccentrics, drowned cats, and the strangely nauseating spectacle of its homely young lead scarfing down a plate of Spaghettios in a bathtub while his mother washed his hair. Mainstream critics cried *"foul!"* while Korine's own generation (he was 23 when he made *Gummo*) placed the video on their staff picks racks[98] and eagerly awaited Korine's next effort.

---

[98] *Gummo* was also among the most stolen video titles! Along with Tinto Brass's *Caligula* (1979), *Gummo* was the most-stolen video title in First Run Video's rental library.

Needless to say, Korine's films aren't for everyone. True to his own muse and Dogma 95's seal of approval, Korine's *Julien Donkey-Boy* cultivates a home-movie (or, more accurately, a home video) look from end to end, shot on a variety of current video filmmaking technologies to immerse the viewer into the reality of the titular character, a schizophrenic young man simmering in the venomous juices of his New Jersey home. In the opening moments, Julien (Scottish actor Ewan Bremner of *Naked*, 1993, *Trainspotting*, 1996, *Snatch*, 2000, etc.) lashes out at a young boy (Brian Fisk) over the discovery of a turtle, and apparently kills the boy, though one can't be sure, any more than Julien can be sure of what he's doing, done, or may do. Basing the character on his own (currently institutionalized) Uncle Eddy (to whom the film is dedicated), Korine intends to plunge us into an utterly unromanticized vicarious experience of schizophrenia; though we do not literally see the film through Julien's eyes (indeed, we are occasionally privileged to see events Julien does not), it is clearly his perspective of the world we are sharing.

There have been other subjective evocations of schizophrenia, such as Lodge Kerrigan's terrifying *Clean, Shaven* (1993), but Korine saturates us in Julien's day-to-day life with an engaging immediacy fostered by the very medium of video. The intimacy is painful, not only for the most obviously abrasive aspects of Julien's existence, but also for its unexpected beauties and tenderness. Julien's father (played, or inhabited, by German director Werner Herzog at his most arrogant) is a tyrant, constantly berating, belittling, and brutalizing the rest of the family, reserving his worst bile for Julien's brother Chris (Evan Neumann of *Liberty Heights*, 1999). They're all mad, save perhaps for Julien's sister Pearl

(Chloë Sevigny of *Kids*, 1995, *Trees Lounge*, 1996, *Boys Don't Cry*, 1999, *American Psycho*, 2000, etc.), whose loving nature and genuine affection for Julien seems the only ripple of possible redemption in the suburban hell Korine captures. In a touching scene, Pearl speaks to Julien over the phone pretending to be their deceased mother: she understands Julien's madness, his needs, and the small indulgences that can offer a fleeting emotional oasis. As the film unreels ('unreals'?), however, Pearl's fragile predicament asserts itself: she is not spared her father's occasional tyranny, but the question of who might be the father of her unborn child and the family's apparent apathy about the matter becomes increasingly troubling.

Though a rough chronology inevitably asserts itself — the film does build to a genuinely wrenching final act — *Julien Donkey-Boy* refutes any attempt at narrative cohesion. Korine deliberately fragments the chronology with flourishes that occasionally push the parameters of the professed Dogma 95 'rules': filtered imagery, editing techniques, and video effects (including at least one superimposition of one image upon another) are certainly special effects of a kind, and imposed upon the otherwise stark verisimilitude of the film.

There is also the issue of the occasional eccentrics and 'human oddities' Korine brings into the fray: an armless card-shark neighbor (Alvin Law) who infuriates Julien's father, and is later shown playing drums; an albino African-American rap-artist (Victor Varnado, who was less tastefully cast as a homeless acolyte of the devil himself in *End of Days*, 1999[99]); a magician (Tom Mullica) whose outrageous cigarette-devouring antics stop

---

[99] See *Blur, Vol. 2*, pp. 47-49.

the film dead for a few minutes of comic relief amid the melancholy and despair. Though the presence of such eccentrics arguably grounds the performances of the film — Ewan Bremner is excellent as Julien, but he is, after all, an actor playing a role — and creates a suburban universe in which the madness of Julien's entire family is merely another mutation, or permutation, of skewed, false 'normality,' there is something exploitative about such casting. It is, however, already part and parcel of Korine's body of work. Korine peopled *Gummo* with similar curios and oddities, a directorial quirk arguably closer to the spirit of Tod Browning, Alejandro Jodorowsky, and John Waters than the Dogma 95 manifesto (though Von Trier may have sanctioned this practice with the Downes' Syndrome dishwashers of *The Kingdom*, who act as a pair of 'Greek Chorus' narrators throughout that chilling epic).

Like many Dogma 95 efforts, *Julien Donkey-Boy* is a calculated assault on the very notion of film-as-entertainment. You aren't *meant* to be entertained or amused, but submerged and challenged. This is an ugly, distressing, depressing work; but it's also a engaging, fascinating *sui generis* work, and once seen, it is impossible to forget.

Not all Dogma 95 acolytes are so opposed to the fine art of storytelling and the seductive pull of genre, however, as demonstrated by Lars Von Trier's latest masterwork, ***DANCER IN THE DARK*** (2000). Danish director Lars Von Trier is undoubtably the best-known of the Dogma 95 founding fathers. Eschewing mainstream 1990s studio filmmaking and his own early complex, multi-layered works (*The Element of Crime/Forbrydelsens Element*, 1984; *Zentropa/Europa*,

1991) to create a more immediate, primal form of cinema, Von Trier has nevertheless embraced genre conventions and situations if only to relentlessly dissect and subvert them. Thus, the hospital soap operatics and ghost story trappings of *The Kingdom* and *The Kingdom II* opens with an uneasy blend of familiar medical-television intrigues and old-fashioned spectral shenanigans, only to mutate into an utterly hilarious autopsy of corrupt modern medicine fused with a shivery haunting that spawns the most hideous infant (Udo Kier) in the history of cinema. *Breaking the Waves* ravaged cozy romantic tragedies and inspirational religious 'miracle' parables with the tale of the sexual awakening, debasement, and martyrdom of an innocent Scottish woman (Emily Watson) who communes with God to — and beyond — the bitter end.

Von Trier, ever the provocateur, once again pushes the envelope with misanthropic glee in *Dancer in the Dark*, gutting the conventions of the movie musical to plunge yet another innocent waif (played with radiant clarity by Icelandic pop singer Björk Guðmundsdóttir, *aka* Björk) into an unflinching confrontation with soul-crushing evil. To that end, Von Trier shamelessly embraces the hoariest of melodramatic cliches: an impoverished Czech immigrant Selma (Björk) is going blind in a deceptively benign American Northwest of the early 1960s, holding on to her factory job to raise money for an operation to save her son Gene (Vladica Kostic) from the same genetic condition.

Selma is a wayward waif, a child-woman struggling to raise her son in an inhospitable world. Her simple desires and plans unravel in a heartbreaking scenario as her real blindness to the ways of the world exacts a terrible toll: she saves her meager earnings in a tin can instead of the bank, she trusts and confides in the wrong man, and continues to pretend she can see well enough to operate dangerous machinery en route to yet another searing Von Trier martyrdom. Every step into the abyss, Selma loses herself in musical reveries, imaginary songs and dances (staged by Vincent Paterson, who choreographed music videos like Michael Jackson's 1988 *Moonwalker* and features including *Evita* and *The Birdcage*, both 1996) that brighten the darkest corners of Selma's existence (the factory, a train trestle, a courtroom, etc.).

At one point in the grim proceedings, Selma says, *"When I used to work in a factory, I used to dream that I was in a musical, because in a musical nothing dreadful ever happens."* Ah, but *this* is a Von Trier musical. Dreadful things indeed happen, culminating in a harrowing attack on capital punishment utterly appropriate to this second President Bush regime. If, at the peak of their skills, Polish novelist Jerzy Kosinski had scribed a musical for Polish director Roman Polanski, it might have resembled Von Trier's brilliant masterwork. More to the point, British playwright and screenwriter Dennis Potter blazed similar trails in *The Singing Detective* (TV miniseries 1986[100]) and *Pennies From Heaven* (TV miniseries 1978; filmed in 1981) with dystopian intensity.

The naturalistic settings and sounds into which Selma's musical fantasies erupt superficially recall the dour 'anti-musical' antics of Peter Bogdanovich's *They All Laughed* (1981), Woody Allen's *Everyone Says I Love You* (1996), or Robert Altman's *Popeye* (my all-time favorite 'anti-musical'). Unlike the Bogdanovich or

---

[100] *The Singing Detective* was adapted into a feature film in 2003, after this essay was written and published.

Allen, however, Von Trier places Selma's imagined interludes amid banal realities with a purpose: to simultaneously celebrate and stripmine the musical in all its vainglorious lunacy.

Ever since Busby Berkeley shamelessly choreographed *"We're in the Money"* for Depression-era audiences in Mervyn LeRoy's *Gold Diggers of 1933* (1933), American musicals have channeled cultural fantasies of relief, reward, and redemption with absurdist optimism. Von Trier embraces the seductive power of the musical form (using music, song, and dance to express that which the characters could not or would not otherwise express) while surgically exposing its madness. In her off hours, Selma labors in a local community theater production of *The Sound of Music*, aching to win a key part or perform one of her favorite tunes; well and good, but working a late-night shift in the factory, Selma lapses into a rousing dance fantasy fueled by the industrial rhythms of the workplace, risking dire injury to herself and others while lost in the dream musical extravaganza. Infused by Björk's potent music and bewitching presence, Von Triers' and Vincent Paterson's minimalist song and dance numbers elegantly wed Selma's own naivete, exuberance, and despair (the surprise presence of Joel Grey — the original emcee of Bob Fosse's *Cabaret*, filmed in 1972 — in the penultimate dance number is a bonus). Mark Bell's collaborative compositions find music in the cold, concrete echoes of her surroundings: music emerges from the clang of steel, the stroke of a train engine, the scratching of a court artist's pencil.

As the film proceeds into deeper life-and-death jeopardy, the fantasies become more extreme: celebrating her blindness, bringing the dead to life, hallucinating succor, support, and redemption where there is none.

Just as musicals have often done in the broader cultural context, Selma's musical interludes try to undo damage done, fantasize escape routes where there is no exit, all the while embodying a longing for a better life and lovelier, more loving world.

To capture this clash of harsh reality and ever-optimistic fantasy with the desired immediacy, Von Trier stretched the rules of Dogma 95. Supplanting the artifice of MGM sound stages and Busby Berkeley delirium was an ambitious application of cutting-edge video technology in the hopes of capturing the musical numbers live in a single take, using one hundred strategically-positioned cameras (!), elaborate technical support, and months of editing to shape the hundreds of hours of raw footage into a coherent whole. Thus, one generation's artifice arguably gave way to another; then again, the rules of Dogma 95 were made to be broken by its iconoclastic founders. As Von Trier pragmatically admits at the conclusion of the *Dancer in the Dark* DVD special feature *"100 Cameras,"* his conceit of filming *all* the musical numbers live simply didn't work *"because we had to cut from different takes."* These sequences are, nonetheless, intoxicating and utterly true to the tenor of the film.

Whether he is a visionary or a monster, Von Trier demonstrates anew the power of the Dogma 95 aesthetic. He knows the world can and does crush lives and souls, and exposes how we cling to hope in the worst of circumstances. Part of the fascination here is the increasingly cruel clash between Von Trier's pragmatic misanthropy and Björk's seemingly bottomless passion and lifeforce; it is, indeed, the soul of the film. A similar dynamic fueled *Beneath the Waves*, as Emily Watson embraced prostitution in a perverse quest to slake and save her crippled husband. Björk described working on *Dancer in the Dark* as being *"very painful... like signing on to war, going to the Vietnam War. I believed I might die."*[101] One can't help but think of Alfred Hitchcock's now-notorious cinematic love-and-hate relations with iconic blondes like Kim Novak, Grace Kelly, Janet Leigh, and Tippi Hedren, pitching them into the direst scenarios imaginable (and, at his most extreme, subjecting Hedren to traumatizing days of genuine physical abuse to film the concluding attack of *The Birds* in 1963). Though her *Dancer in the Dark* pains earned her the coveted Palme d'Or for best actress at Cannes and Golden Globe and Academy Award nominations, Björk has sworn off acting hereafter.

This only fueled the critical backlash against the film, though there's no denying that Von Trier has once again engaged with his chosen medium and genre to dissect and reanimate them with Frankensteinian zeal. By doing so, Von Trier unveils how and why these genres — war films (*Zentropa*), romance and religious films (*Breaking the Waves*), horror films (*The Kingdom I* and *II*), and now musicals — are so vital to us by making the implicit explicitly seen, heard, and felt.

Selma's almost pathetic obsession with musicals personifies our own collective cultural link with the genre. By the final act of *Dancer in the Dark*, Von Trier and Björk vividly remind us that music is a lifeline — perhaps *the* life line. Through their collaborative art, they remind us that the very beat of our heart is our only tenuous bridge between the light of redemption and the

---

[101] Quoted from *"Björk's Big Adventure,"* Premiere, October 2000, page 84.

darkness of the pit... and just how fragile, and precious, it truly is.

(Dancer in the Dark is rated a very strong 'R' for dramatic and emotional intensity, adult situations, and violence.) [102]

---

[102] This was originally published as a two-part article; I have slightly revised the published version to consolidate it into single essay. Only the transitional passages have been revised; this is the definitive version.

About the Author

Stephen R. Bissette is world renowned for his 30+ years of work in comics (*Saga of the Swamp Thing, Taboo, 1963, Tyrant*, etc.) and now savors life as an artist, writer, lecturer and instructor. His latest comic story appeared in the anthology *Secrets & Lies* (Magic Inkwell Press, 2008) and he recently co-authored *Prince of Stories: The Many Worlds of Neil Gaiman* with Hank Wagner and Christopher Golden for St. Martin's Press. He presently teaches at the Center for Cartoon Studies in White River Jct., VT, and lives in Windsor, VT with his wife Marjory. Visit his website at www.srbissette.com

S.R. Bissette's Blur, Volume 1 and *Volume 2* are also available from Black Coat Press.

www.ingramcontent.com/pod-product-compliance
Lightning Source LLC
Chambersburg PA
CBHW022100160426
43198CB00008B/295